AND THERE I STOOD WITH MY PICCOLO

MEREDITH WILLSON *And There I Stood With My Piccolo*

UNIVERSITY OF MINNESOTA PRESS   MINNEAPOLIS · LONDON

Originally published in 1948 by Doubleday and Company, Inc.
First University of Minnesota Press edition, 2009

Published by the University of Minnesota Press
111 Third Avenue South, Suite 290
Minneapolis, MN 55401-2520
http://www.upress.umn.edu

LIBRARY OF CONGRESS CATALOGING-IN-PUBLICATION DATA
Willson, Meredith, 1902–1984.
And there I stood with my piccolo / Meredith Willson. — 1st
University of Minnesota Press ed.
    p. cm.
Originally published in 1948 by Doubleday and Company, Inc.
ISBN 978-0-8166-6769-7 (pb : alk. paper)
1. Willson, Meredith, 1902–1984. 2. Composers—United States—
Biography. I. Title.
ML410.W714A3 2009
780.92—dc22
[B]   2009016767

Printed in the United States of America on acid-free paper
The University of Minnesota is an equal-opportunity educator and
employer.

22 21 20 19 18 17   10 9 8 7 6 5 4 3

To MY RINI

An old Moravian flute player once told me a story that went like this:

"A very important king hired a whole orchestra to play for him one night during his supper, just because he felt lonesome.

"This orchestra played great and the king was so delighted that before going to bed he said, 'Boys, your playing gave me the whips and jingles, and just for that you can all go to my countinghouse and fill your instruments with gold pieces.'

"I can still hear that happy clatter as sack after sack of golden tiddlies streamed into the tuba and slithered down the neck of the bassoon and spilled out over the bells of the French horns.

"And there I stood with my piccolo."

AND THERE I STOOD WITH MY PICCOLO

1. NEW YORK TALK WAS A HECK OF A shock to me. So were mountains. You can read about things all your life and still be completely unprepared for what they actually turn out to be. At any rate, I certainly wasn't prepared for Pennsylvania, all full of mountains like what I saw out of the Pullman window that morning, and I can still hear the Western Union kids that swarmed over the train as we pulled into Manhattan Transfer. "Teleegrams to all pernts," with a metallic zing that sounded like a straight mute in a two-dollar trumpet.

Sounds stay in your memory longer than anything else, it seems to me. The older I get, the clearer I can hear the sounds that were the dimensions of the world during my first seven or eight years in it back in Mason City. Sounds like Mama scraping the burnt toast downstairs while you're hurrying into your "ironclad" stockings and your "underwaist"—that little harness affair with all the buttons on it. And the particular sound of your front door opening in the winter and the screen door slamming in summer, and Papa's derby hitting the newel post in the front hall, almost a dead heat with the six o'clock whistle you could hear all the way from the roundhouse, and "The Toreador Song" on the music box while you had to take your afternoon nap.

Sunday naps were different. The street sounds in front would be quieter—more sedate, sort of. A walking horse would pass by and you'd fall asleep, doubling up the tempo in your mind to make it sound like he was galloping. The illusion was perfect, except it took him so long to get up to Brice's corner that you knew he must be walking after all.

Sunday sounds always began with Mama playing "Jerusalem the Golden" and "Jesus Wants Me for a Sunbeam," or maybe "The Church in the Wildwood," on the black upright piano in the parlor, while my brother Cedric and I were brushing the snow off "Little Nemo" and "Buster Brown and Tige" and trying to figure out how to keep from going to Sunday school.

You could hear Mr. Sale shoveling off his walk next door—a big tinny snow-shovel sound for a drifty, sunny, sparkling snowfall, and a hard scrapy coal-shovel sound for a gloomy hard-packed freeze. There was a difference in the sound of lawn mowers too. Ours always sounded different from Mr. Sale's on account of he had a canvas thing on the back to catch the grass and we didn't.

The autumn sounded like coal going down the chute through the basement window into the coalbin, and spring sounded like the click of a peewee dropped into your marble box, or one of Papa's carnelians knocking a glassy or a commie across the sidewalk. There was smooth roller-skate sound across the street in front of Glanville's house where it was new cement, and rough roller-skate sound in front of our house where the cement was old and coarse.

Summer mornings sounded like beating rugs and washtub handles hitting against the sides of the tub filled with ice and covered with old carpet, which my brother Cedric lugged out to the curb where he had his pop stand. Summer five o'clock always sounded like coleslaw chopping in the wooden bowl for supper, and the big wooden potato masher pounding the beefsteak.

Saturdays sounded like the soft-water pump in the cellar—my brother Cedric pumping his hundred strokes, reminding my sinking heart that I had my hundred strokes yet to pump.

Happy sounds were Mr. Hermanson's milk wagon, and Mama's "Hoo-hoo" on Thursdays, which meant she was home from the Sorosis Club with a little cup of nuts or candies knotted in her handkerchief for us kids; the scrunch, as you took a juicy bite out of a stalk of fresh pieplant all nice and dirty from rubbing it in a fistful of Grampa's rock salt out of the salt barrel in the barn; the after-school sounds of erasers being banged together and the "squish" of the soundless door to the public library.

Gloomy sounds were Papa's shaking down the ashes out of the grate down-cellar, reminding you that come Saturday you have to struggle with them through the back-yard snowdrifts to the ash pile. And gloomiest of all, one bell from the schoolhouse tower. Late again.

There were four big white-framed pictures of The Voyage of Life that hung in the parlor, casting a sort of lugubrious warning every time anyone walked into that part of the house. They hung in series on the wall just over the chair with the platform rockers and the springs that made such a perfect hiding place for Easter eggs.

The first picture was a sort of Grecian gondola going out into the river that lay ahead. A little baby lay in the boat, and peacefully floating overhead in a cloud was his Better Self, or I guess maybe his Guardian Angel.

In the second picture the baby was a grown young man, standing fiercely in the bow, heading his frail craft into a terrible storm with thunder and lightning. His Guardian Angel was shaking a finger at him from his cloud, urging him not to risk the storm and the rough water ahead, but it was obvious that the young man was not paying any heed.

In the third picture did he make a mistake, oh, brother, but his Guardian Angel pulled him out of it, and in the fourth he was an old man with whiskers and he and his boat were headed into a very calm and serene stream, while G. Angel waited far off in the distance in the clouds, in the middle of a bunch of snow-white turrets and towers and palaces and stuff.

I guess worrying about that young fellow's boat trip did me more good than harm though. G. A. picked me out a real nice "boat" and a set of patient neighbors right off the bat, which was particularly important, since making music was all I did around the house, except, of course, play one old cat with my brother Cedric and my cousin Phil.

We never fought as much as other kids because just as we got excited about the game my aunt Mae would yell for Phil to come in and treadle. She used to get tired working the sewing machine and about three o'clock every day Phil had to go in and crawl under the machine and— well—treadle.

My mother was superintendent of the Sunday

school, so I had to be in all the Sunday-school cantatas and wear black velvet pants. In fact, my earliest memory is about the Sunday school and Charlie Rau, who ran the stereopticon.

He had painted the Star of Bethlehem on a slide and at Christmas time would point the machine in every direction to make the star travel across the ceiling of the church, down the wall, and finally end up over the choir loft. There Avis Stott would stand and sing "Joy to the World," combining glorious music, showmanship, and electrical magic enough to set my little four-year-old cork a-bobbin' with the first real thrill that I can remember.

Mr. Rau liked to have my brother Cedric hand him the different slides, and we always felt so important, after the opening organ music, to hear Mr. Rau's voice booming out, "Will Cedric Willson please come to the balcony!"

Like any Iowa child, I loved to play circus and hated to practice the piano. I hung around the bandstand in the summertime and practically passed out when they played "Custer's Last Stand" with the red fire and everything. Naturally I wanted to play in the band someday, and that got me to dreaming about Sousa's band and show business.

My first experience on the stage was when I was six and it was rather discouraging. They needed some kids down at the Princess Theatre, and Mama was cleaning the attic that particular Saturday morning, so I sneaked off to fame and fortune.

It was bad enough to have to get into a frog suit and hop around, but when they told me I also had to put two wires from a flashlight battery into my mouth and bite them together to make the frog's eyes flash on and off, I would have quit, excepting that I had already accepted the fee—my first penny.

I learned something about the value of money when I took this penny into the Candy Kitchen and pointed out some fancy chocolate creams through the glass. Mr. Skondrus took my penny and handed me one chocolate.

Even the silver paper around it didn't change the bottomless dismay that poured into my stomach, that frantic what-have-I-done feeling; but I was ashamed to say, "Mr. Skondrus, I thought I was gonna get a sackful. Here's your candy. Can I have my penny back?"

I don't remember ever eating that piece of candy, but I do remember standing outside the store, numb with horror and soaked with tears at the way I had dissipated my treasure. But not for all the candy in the world would I have gone back inside. I always did my shopping at the grocery-store candy counter after that.

Mama had always said, "After you get so you can play the piano real nice, you must learn to play another instrument so you will stand out among the others boys when you go to school."

This sounded like a logical start toward Sousa's band, so Mama scraped up the money (isn't it wonderful how mamas always seem to be able to "scrape up the money"?) and we sent away to the Chicago Mail Order House for a flute!

Such goings on and hysterical unwrapping of paper you have never seen in your whole born days as that Saturday morning when my cousin Walter, who was the postman on our street, brought the package from Chicago. And what a horrible disappointment to get the flute out finally and put it together and discover that instead of holding this instrument in front of you, as I had always imagined (there never having been a flute in Mason City before), you had to play it sideways, practically over your shoulder, where you couldn't possibly see what was going on.

After Cousin Walter explained how complicated it would be to sign the different things and wrap up the flute again and mail it back to Chicago, we finally decided it was more trouble to send it back than to keep it. So I kept it and started to take lessons from a gentleman who actually played the cornet but who managed to stay one lesson ahead of me on the flute.

My mother had taught me all the piano she knew and had turned me over to Ed Patchen, the organist at the Congregational Church, but he was so good-natured that I missed more lessons than I took.

When I didn't show up, Mr. Patchen would just toss off his favorite cuss word, "my conscience," and go downstairs to the pool hall and shoot a game of billiards with Bert Avery, whose right eye was a little off center but who played a remarkable game just the same.

Mr. Avery explained this by saying, "I size up the shot pretty close and then shut my eyes and whale away. Surprise you how many of 'em you can make."

One morning as I came downstairs to breakfast my father was singing "Tipperary" and my sister Dixie was faking a sort of alto part along with him. Well, I jumped in on the baritone an octave higher, and lo and behold, I had discovered for the first time, that I could fake a harmony part myself. The world seemed to open up with every exciting first time like that.

How well I remember my first ice cream cone. "The man down at the corner by the bank sells ice cream in a little glass and you can eat the glass!" And my first street carnival was all Ferris wheel and butterfly scarf dancers making swirls in colored lights.

Imagine a girly-girly show in a street carnival today, with the sole idea being to show that it's beautiful to wave silk scarves around in red, green, yellow, and blue old-style acetylene spotlights. I'm glad I remember a bunch of small-town Iowans standing in a tent across from the post office on a balmy June night in 1915 being thrilled by just colors and kimono skirlings.

And my first moving picture, *The Highwayman* —the forest fire part was photographed on red film, of course.

But even more wonderful was my first kaleidoscope—not the kind you twist, like a horizontal cocktail shaker, but a little wooden slide for your magic lantern with a tiny crank sticking out. You put the slide in and turned the crank and that was better than any technicolor movie I've ever seen.

I remember our regular magic-lantern slides too—a series of adventures of little German-looking boys who always fell in the water or something. The colors were always sort of thick, like the transfer pictures we used to stick on the backs of our hands.

My first shrimp Papa brought home in a can. We were circumspect, as it seems to me, about the little black string of a stomach running around the shrimp. My first grapefruit—load 'er up with sugar and it was just barely swallerable. My first radishes Papa pulled in the morning—to have with his coffee for breakfast.

And my first day at the public library I spent discovering the *White Fairy Book,* the *Green Fairy Book,* and a horrible depressing little quickie, something about the GOOPS. This was my first awed participation in the card-stamping ceremony at the big circular desk in front, with the ink pads and stamping things and the long pencils with little metal date attachments fastened on the side, down near the point. I remember the meticulous way my card would be taken out of its slot and put back, properly and legally stamped, and the book officially handed to me amidst all the muffled sounds and whispers; and the first time I was told that the big rock on the library corner was a meteor that actually fell out of the sky.

Later on came things like my first astonished look at the man on Main Street sitting at his little table with his special side-winder pen, writing calling cards with flowers and birds and flourishes.

And then there was my first time away from home and my first piccolo. When summer vacation came around after my freshman year in high school I was hired to play the flute in the orchestra at Lake Okoboji, a hundred miles or so from Mason City. The season lasted eight weeks and I was expected to double on the piccolo.

Down I tore to Vance's store and thumbed

hastily through the catalogue. There she was—a little beauty—silver-plated with gold keys, all for ninety-six dollars. I arranged to buy her at twelve dollars a week, which, by an unusual coincidence, was the exact amount of my weekly salary at Lake Okoboji, although I got my room and board thrown in.

This summer resort was also the scene of my first sex faux pas. We were sitting on the veranda with a couple of girls and, there being a bit of a lull, I naturally spoke up. Having nothing better to say, I started to read aloud the announcements on the bulletin boards: "Special prizes for the costume dance Saturday night," and so on, and so on, till I ran head-on into "Lost: A lady's handbag in the ladies'——"

Well, I was terrified, of course, for obviously I couldn't say "toilet" out loud, and just leaving it up in the air would be even worse. So in a decreasing hangdog accent I ended weakly with, "In the ladies'—er—uh—handbag!"

A long silence fell over the veranda, and this is the first time I've referred to the incident since.

During the last week up at Okoboji, the leader, a violinist named Emery Moore, had to go to war. Our orchestra consisted of piano, drums, cornet, trombone, clarinet, and me, the flute and piccolo. Well, you couldn't play violin parts very well on a trombone, cornet, clarinet, or drums, so the logical substitute for the violin was a flute, and I became the leader for the last Saturday-night dance of the season.

Of course I had to stand up to start off the orchestra and I was so relieved when the first number was over and we all finished together that I sank heavily down into my chair right onto the piccolo. Being metal, it curved into my "seat contour" and became part scimitar and part bow and arrow—but no longer piccolo. You can't straighten out a bent piccolo, and I had just that afternoon put the last twelve-dollar money order into the mail. Anyway, I learned to swim that summer.

My first kiss is fixed well in my memory too. This happened somewhat before I learned to pucker on the flute, and at the risk of being considered an ordinary cad I will tell you that her name was Feril Hawkes. Where her mother got that name I don't know, but I will also tell you that her sisters were named Tempy and Vitell. Anyway, she was seven and I was eight, and though I know it is not at all plausible at that age, yet I distinctly remember taking her to the Airdrome, an open-air hunk of scaffolding that was one of Mason City's first theaters, to take in a personal appearance of John L. Sullivan. We had grocery-store chocolates and stopped in the lumberyard on the way home and bussed each other on the cheek. Forgive me, Feril, but gosh, you were so pretty and I was so young.

Then my first 10-20-30 drama at the Princess Theatre some years later. My brother and I went with our ashes money which we dropped so regularly down the cold-air register in the hall at home that we kept the stepladder down there inside the hole.

Stark life was in that drama about the wayward daughter who was turned, with her shame, out of the house forever by her forthright parents. I realized some years later the reason my brother didn't explain that part of the play to me was because he didn't understand it either, even though Mama was by this time reading aloud a chapter nightly of *What Every Young Man Should Know*, but we both always fell asleep.

I sure went for the drama of the second-act curtain that day, however, which I *did* understand. The hero was speaking to the brakeman. We in the audience knew the brakeman was the "heavy" and a phony. "What is the time, sir?" questions Jack.

"A quarter to eleven," the villain answers.

Quick as a flash Handsome Jack thunders, "You're no railroad man or you'd 'a' said ten forty-five!" (APPLAUSE.)

I had a real flute teacher by this time named Squiz Hazelton who had come to Mason City with a musical show. Squiz found out I could fake, so he suggested my doubling on the banjo. Before long I had my first taste of trouping with the local dance orchestra. We would play nearby towns like Lyle, Minnesota, and Britt, and Belle Plaine. And I can still see our drummer, Ralph Kelso, coming around the corner of the depot in the middle of the night, being hit by a hunk of Minnesota blizzard right smack in the bass drum which he had on his back. He sailed away like an iceboat, and we picked him up two blocks down the street just in time to build a fire in the middle of the Milwaukee Railroad tracks, which was the accepted way to stop a train in a small town in those days.

I was playing in the eleven-piece high school orchestra, too, and we practiced in each other's homes every other Tuesday night. The instrumentation was not exactly ideal, but we took what we could get, which included Marion Maguire playing the cello parts on her euphonium. Our program was usually the "Crusader Overture," Beethoven's "Minuet," "Our Director March," a dish of blancmange and a couple Nabiscos, then Schubert's "Serenade" and the long walk home just in time to hear the courthouse clock strike ten.

Anyhow, I did graduate from Mason City High School in spite of a pretty horrible song

I wrote for my class, and off I went to New York with Papa's fried chicken, Mama's prayers, a mail-order flute under my arm, and a bent piccolo in my pocket.

2. I LEARNED TO EAT RAW OYSTERS IN New York. New York, like oysters, is also an acquired taste, it seems to me. Once you bluff the town out of that upper-classman-in-a-world-of-freshmen superiority, and expose its imitation cold-heartedness, you never get it out of your system.

I guess everybody's first oyster is an experience. Mine was in Shanley's Restaurant in Times Square. I had always thought salt came in an honest upstanding salt shaker, so when I saw a little silver salt dish in front of me I naturally thought it was something for the oysters. I selected the wrong fork, rolled the oyster lightly in the salt dish, and stuck it in my mouth; and, human nature being what it is, I even managed to smile appreciatively at the waiter, who was looking at me in a kind of fascinated horror.

Hugheses are like Willsons in the respect that practically all Hugheses are related. Of three celebrated ones (Rush, Howard, and Rupert) I know two: Rupert and Rush.

Rush once told me about his first oyster. It happened when he was six and he was at a party. He'd been sitting at the table for some time without saying a word, when the hostess noticed there was only one oyster gone from his plate. She said, "Rush dear, don't you want the rest of your oysters?"

Rush answered without opening his mouth, "I 'on't eben want '*ish* one."

I know a little girl who was brought up near the White Sea who never learned to like oysters at all because her father once told her that oysters go "peep" as you swallow them.

3. OF COURSE THE MAIN IDEA OF GOING to New York, aside from the forlorn hope of getting my piccolo straightened, was to study the flute with the world-famous flutist, the great Georges Barrère. He lived on Ninety-third Street near the Drive, and I was sure nervous on the way to his house on account of I'd been dreaming of studying the flute with him ever since the vague images of being a fireman, a great surgeon, a lawyer, and a bank president became lost in the realization that I was turning into a flute player.

Mr. Barrère almost seemed to be expecting me, though, and his year-old blond baby Jean, crawling underfoot the whole time, kind of put me at my ease. We arranged for the lessons and then he phoned several of his real successful pupils like Lem Williams and Billy Kincaid—he's the cherry on top of Ormandy's Philadelphia Symphony— and asked them to help me get a job playing the flute someplace.

They advised me to go to the union every day with my flute under my arm, and sooner or later, they said, somebody would need a flute player in a hurry and might take a chance on me.

Nobody spoke much English at the union. All the Italians gathered in the center under the clock, the Germans by the stairs, and the Russians under the balcony. I couldn't find any Iowans anyplace, so I just circulated, you might say.

One day a man with a wild look in his eye grabbed me and said, "You playa floot? Good. Standa youself under da clock." I waited for three hours and he came back looking sad. "I finda not one floot butta you. You be my sospitute tonight atta da Wint' Gard'."

Well, whadayaknow! Me getting a job to substitute for the flute player at the Winter Garden! I dashed to the nearest Western Union office to send a telegram home to Mason City—PLAYING TONIGHT WINTER GARDEN—and rushed out to find the theater so I wouldn't be late.

I had always thought the Winter Garden was somewhere near Times Square, but the directions the man gave me on a card told me to take the subway to Houston Street, which was hard to find, because I called it *Hugh*ston and all the New Yorkers called it *House*ton.

Anyway, *that* Winter Garden was in the Bowery and not famous at all. It was a combo picture house and burleyque upstairs over a kosher market, and I got home at one o'clock in the morning and found a telegram stuck in the door from Mason City: ALWAYS KNEW YOU'D MAKE GOOD.

But I found another "sospitute" job the next week at the Crescent Theatre on Boston Road in the Bronx, Sol Klein leader. Mr. Klein was very nice to me and gave me the job steady, fifty-two fifty a week, which took care of the flute lessons and also allowed me to sign up for the morning classes at the Damrosch Institute.

Whenever an important picture like *Humoresque* came along Mr. Klein would get the manager to let him augment the orchestra with a few extra musicians. Mr. Halperin was the manager and he did not by any means have a tin ear, since he was always standing in the back, listening to the music.

Whenever the orchestra took an intermission, the pianist stayed in the pit and kept playing. But one time he wanted to get a malted down at Mr. Beitelman's stationery store—best malteds I ever tasted—and I slipped over onto the piano stool to fill in, glad of the chance to try over an exercise in sequence I had to have ready for the next morning's class at the Institute.

I guess the exercise didn't fit the action on the screen any too well because Mr. Halperin came tearing down the aisle and told me—and the people in the first three rows—so. I saved the exercise, however, and used it ten years later as the theme for a piece called "Thoughts while Strolling," dedicated to a remarkable man I was proud to know, named O. O. McIntyre. Mr. McIntyre always wore purple pajamas, and Mrs. McIntyre is a wonderful woman and sends me post cards from places like the deck of the *Empress of India* every once in a while, and Paul Whiteman played the first performance of this piece which eventually came out as a popular song on a Bing Crosby record called "Whose Dream Are You?"

But what I wanted to say was, one time at the Crescent Theatre Mr. Klein wanted to add a viola to the orchestra, and all the good violas were busy, so he just phoned the union and said, "Send me a viola." Answering the call, a nice old gentleman put down the checkerboard and picked up his viola and came to the Crescent Theatre to play with us that week.

He sat next to me in the orchestra pit and played so out of tune I couldn't stand it any more, and I finally leaned over to him and whispered, "If you'll excuse me, your C string is a little flat."

He plucked at the string a couple of times and then said pleasantly, "That's funny. It's about as tight as I usually have it."

In the meantime, I had played for John Philip

Sousa and got the job of first flute with his band. Mr. Klein's mother gave me a fine farewell dinner of stuffed tongue and gefüllte fish. I had scaled the heights, the world was my apple, and nobody will ever feel more important than I did the morning I went down to Brooks Brothers to get measured for my Sousa uniform.

$4.$ DID YOU EVER HEAR OF SAM OTTS? There's no such fellow, you know, yet there are thousands of people who firmly believe the legend that an immigrant boy of that name came to this country some eighty years ago, and that stamped on his trunk, according to legend, were his initials —S. O.—for Sam Otts, followed by the letters U. S. A.—his destination. S-O-U-S-A.

That *could* have been the way Sousa got his name, but it wasn't. John Philip Sousa's name was Sousa, not Sam Otts, and the first time he ever saw the old country was when he was invited there by practically every crowned head in Europe. Pretty good for a barefoot kid from Washington, D.C.

After I joined the band I used to sit on the train every day with a pocket score of the "Nutcracker Suite" just to make an impression on anyone who happened to walk down the aisle. Actually I had no idea how to read a score.

Mr. Sousa suspected this, I'm sure, as I used to stay on one page entirely too long, but instead of asking me embarrassing questions he slid into my seat one day and started giving me little hints about orchestrating and how he got so he could read a score and all.

Believe me, he got so he could write a score too, the most gorgeous marches in the whole world, that's all. No silly little tune with an umpa-umpa accompaniment in any of Sousa's marches. Every part of a Sousa march is inspired—the bass line, the woodwind figures, the trombone counter-melodies, and even the peckhorn afterbeats. Listen to these: "The New York Hippodrome," "Man-hattan Beach," "El Capitan," "The Free Lance," "Powhatan's Daughter," "The Gallant Seventh," "King Cotton," "High School Cadets," "Wash-ington Post," and seventy or eighty more. Why, he couldn't write a bad march if he tried, and there sure ought to be a law against playing "The Stars and Stripes Forever" as a razzle-dazzle com-edy play-off the way you used to hear it in vaude-ville, and the way you still hear it occasionally on the radio.

Anyway, what I wanted to say was, I trouped for three seasons with Sousa from Portland to Portland and from Ottawa to Havana—real two-a-day trouping. If it's possible to play a matinee in Butte and a night in Cheyenne, we did it.

Sousa was a great musician—composed every note of everything he ever put his name on. That seems a horribly obvious remark to make, but lots of people have some cockeyed idea that he paid somebody to help him. Sousa was a good novelist, too, and a mighty fine trapshooter.

We played a matinee on the veranda of the Lancaster Gun Club one time because Mr. Sousa wanted to attend the shoot the following day. The management got the dates mixed, however, and I was right in the middle of my flute solo when somebody yelled, "Pull!" and the celebrated "Godard Waltz" developed into a duet for flute and shotgun.

The Sousa band carried six flute players as standard equipment, and one of them was a round Ingersoll-faced young man from Connecticut by the name of George Ford. He had a bouncing cheerfulness about him and would laugh at anything, but he had absolutely no restraint or control if anything really struck him funny. Whenever we played "The Stars and Stripes Forever," the piccolos all marched down to the footlights for that famous piccolo part, and one time a woman was sitting in the first row of the Denver Auditorium examining us from not more than six feet away through a pair of large field glasses. Well, George started to tremble and quiver and shake and roll and wiggle his fingers helplessly around his sputtering piccolo. It was only a question of time till we all lost control, and for the rest of the piece, there the six of us stood, *hors de combat*, as you might say, doggedly clutching our instruments in playing position, completely unable to make a sound.

In quieter moments George Ford had the fastest triple tongue of any flute player I ever heard. I asked him one day how he learned to do this so well, and his happy face opened like a quarter to three and he said, "Didn't you know I come from Naugatuck, Connecticut? Just say that over a few times every day for ten or twenty years—Naugatuck, Connecticut, Naugatuck, Connecticut, Naugatuck, Connecticut—and you'll develop a tongue like a snake."

All the Sousa bandsmen were fine musicians. The only exception I can think of was a very pleasant soft-spoken man who played the second bass clarinet on tour with Mr. Sousa for five years.

The responsibilities of a second bass clarinetist were not large, particularly on tour, because we played the same program day in and day out. The band manager was a very colorful Dixie trombone player by the name of Jay Sims, who carried a Boston bag at all times with the current *Saturday Evening Post* under the handles, a cigar in his face whenever the trombone wasn't in it, silver-rimmed spectacles, and the makings of a World Series pool in a little black book—or a football pool or whatever happened to be running—in his pocket.

What I was about to say was, Mr. Sims called this second bass clarinet player on the phone at his hotel. I even remember it was in Wheeling, West Virginia. Over the phone Mr. Sims said that Herman Johnson, the first bass clarinet, was suddenly called by illness to his home in Pottstown and so until further notice would Mr. Softspoken please slide over one seat tonight and play the first bass clarinet parts?

"Thank you, Mr. Sims," he said, very softspokenly and pleasantly, and packed his grip and left Wheeling, West Virginia, and not only did not show up at any more concerts, but was never seen again.

As it turned out, this interesting gentleman had been merely holding the instrument for five years, but because of the very mild light tone quality of a bass clarinet and the fact that these particular players sit in an extremely noisy section of the band, and also that there was never such a thing as a second bass clarinet solo, nobody realized that he couldn't play a note! This didn't stop him from cheerfully giving Jay Sims and the Sousa band as references a year later when he applied for a job with the band at Manhattan Beach.

Well—a great variety of things happened during those Sousa band tours. Mr. Sousa had been at it for thirty or more years by the time I joined the band, so nothing ever bothered him—nothing, nothing, nothing.

Even when the scenery fell down in Montgomery, Alabama, he never even glanced up from his music stand. The sousaphones—those big brass basses that twist around your neck like a pretzel and then bell out over your head—were high enough to keep the scenery from falling down completely and killing somebody, probably. So the basses kept playing, "ump—ump—ump—ump," while all the rest of us scrambled and hambled around under the canvas trying to push it back into place.

We first rescued the horn section—the "after-beat" department, as you might say—and of course they chimed right in with the basses as quick as they found their place. So now you heard "umpah —umpah—umpah" instead of just "ump—ump— ump"—and one by one we all got clear of the scenery and came straggling in, so that by the time we hit the last measure we were all playing again.

Mr. Sousa? He turned around and bowed to the terrified audience just as though the scenery was supposed to fall down at every performance. In fact, I distinctly remember we played an encore.

5. THE SOUSA CONTRACT SAID THAT A MEM- ber must wear his uniform at all times, which was kind of like joining the Army. The uniform went all the way up to the Adam's apple. This called for a stiff white collar and stiff white cuffs —presenting a fantastic laundry problem on the road. By the time the second season rolled along, though, a fellow got wise to the "iron cuffs" that all the old troupers wore. They were mostly cellu- loid (although some of them were actually made out of some kind of sheet iron) and snapped right into the sleeves, and it was a cinch to wash them with soap and water every once in a while. The collar to match was sewed right into the uniform, and the white edge that stuck out could be "laun- dered" with the eraser on the end of a pencil. We were always relieved, though, you may be sure, to get to Willow Grove Park near Philadelphia and dig in for a six weeks' summer season and wear civilian clothes at least in the mornings.

This was a remarkable amusement park, this Willow Grove—maybe the oldest park in America—with cinder paths and elaborate flower gardens and water-lily pools that were swept, clipped, manicured, and refreshed three or four times a day. No man could enter the grounds without wearing a coat at all times—no shirt sleeves even in July and August—and the first movie theater in America was built right there on the midway.

We gave four concerts a day, and you may know that Mr. Sousa was pretty unexcited about rehearsals. He'd done all this so many, many times before. So we had a few sketchy hours of rehearsal when we first arrived at the park, and then what the heck, let the chips fall where they may. And we played some difficult stuff, too—orchestra stuff transcribed for band like "The Sorcerer's Apprentice." This is a pretty involved piece to knock off without any rehearsal, and I will never forget our performance of it one summer.

The librarian sent word around that we would make a cut from letter E to letter H, which eliminated about seven minutes of music, also some of the most complicated passages; but this didn't help very much at the concert, for before we had gone very far some of the newer members of the band got completely lost in an avalanche of sixteenth notes, and how we ever finished together I'll never know. As usual, Mr.

Sousa didn't turn a hair and of course we played an encore.

Back in the locker room at the intermission, I overheard a couple of new boys talking it over. "Wasn't it horrible?" said one.

"Yeah," said his friend, "but think how much worse it would have been if we hadn't made that cut."

"Cut?" said the first kid. "What cut?"

Every Sousa season closed with a grand super concert at Madison Square Garden, and it was a tradition among Sousa bandsmen, wherever they might be, to dig out their old Sousa uniforms and show up at that annual concert. We had at least four hundred men in the augmented band the first time I played at the Garden, and when we went down front for "The Stars and Stripes Forever" that was *it*.

First the piccolos went down to the footlights for the piccolo variation—there were sixteen of us —and in just thirty-two measures we were joined by practically all the trumpets and trombones in the music business.

Nearly everybody had played with Mr. Sousa one time or another, and that night there were forty trumpets blasting out the melody on one side, we piccolo players in the middle, thirty trombones playing the countermelody on the other side, and twenty drummers in the back with that rolling Sousa rhythm.

Standing on my right was Ellis McDiarmid from the Cincinnati Symphony and one of the best flute players I ever knew, and next to me on the other side was the first trombone of the Philadelphia Symphony, Simon Mantia, and next to him was Arthur Pryor, the same Arthur Pryor who had his own world-famous band by this time. His old Sousa uniform was slightly moth-eaten and the sleeves nearly up to his elbows. His head was high and his eyes were shining with a couple of tears, I believe.

6. JUST THINK, TOMORROW'S KIDS WON'T know anything about the thrill of hearing Sousa's band. I hope the new button-pushing, streamlined, jet-propelled, atomic-powered age won't also eliminate things like hammers and flatirons.

Wouldn't it be horrible to grow up without ever having cracked black walnuts with the flatiron? We had two flatirons at our house with only one handle—a detachable one that had a little thing to press so you could release the cold iron and pick up the hot one—and, looking back, it seems to me that the biggest comfort of my whole childhood—next to the flannel rag with bacon grease safety-pinned around my neck whenever I had a cold—was that big old friendly, kind family hammer.

Through the years its claws pried open all the exciting Wells Fargo Express boxes, like pecans from Uncle B.B., maple sugar from Sears Roebuck, the Flexible Flyer and the post-card projector and the flute from Chicago. And those claws pulled the nails out of the tree house in order to build the fort, and out of the fort to make the steering device for the pushmobile, and out of the pushmobile to build the clubhouse "down over the hill," and out of the clubhouse to build the stage for the Rose Theatre down-cellar, admission one cent (will settle for six pins).

We spent more time making the pushmobile "steer" than we did riding in it, and more time making the theater curtain roll and unroll than we did acting.

All our plays called for a gun to be fired from ambush on account of this allowed us to simulate rifle smoke by blowing talcum powder onto the stage through the prop rifle barrel as it protruded from the wings—a highly dramatic effect.

We named the Rose Theatre after Mama, hoping to get a little special consideration on carpet-beating days. Mama had played the lead in a great many local productions when she was a belle around Brighton, Illinois, and she tried to give us some histrionic coaching. *Lady Audley's Secret* was Mama's big role, and although we were impressed with her scrapbook and all, we were too filled with that native impatience, so characteristic of the New World, to settle down and learn a few principles.

Now I guess I don't have to say that I'm not one of the look-how-much-better-they-do-it-in-Europe type of Americans. But I gotta point out that we've always been too quick to rush out onto the stage, fumble around by trial and error, and just get by. That's how a lot of us spent the years when we should have been hitting the ball in the rigid confines of a conservatory someplace.

Gershwin, for instance, never learned to orchestrate till he had already composed the "Rhapsody in Blue" and the "Piano Concerto in F." I know, I know—of course "he did all right," but he might have left the world some four hundred-odd symphonies like Papa Haydn instead of a handful of beautiful melodies. However, that's America, and I guess our impulsiveness has paid off in the production world, and as for the artistic end—we're learning, we're learning.

Mama also tried to get us to study up and memorize some dialogue. She bought us *Handy Andy* and *Madison's Budget*, but we preferred just to roll up the curtain, fire a talcum-powder volley, ad lib a couple lines, fall dead, and call it a scene.

No, a hammer is a wonderful thing all right, and that includes the sledge hammer of the circus roustabouts. Boy, was anything more exciting than seeing ten of those giants circle a four-foot tent stake and sledge 'er down into the ground like pushing a candle into a chocolate cake?

Please—you Thomas A. Edisons of tomorrow —please leave room for sledge hammers and family claw hammers and flatirons.

$7.$ BETWEEN SEASONS WITH SOUSA I PLAYED in the Rialto Theatre orchestra. Everybody at the Rialto was pretty excited all right when on one particular occasion Victor Herbert wrote the music for a very elaborate series of tableaux and came in person to conduct the orchestra that week. All of us musicians in New York had a real affection and admiration for this great man, and also he was very amusing at rehearsals on account of, as everybody knows, he was Irish and very witty.

A couple of us were sitting in his dressing room one day egging him on to tell a couple of jokes, when a frightened-looking little man all full of apologies came bowing and scraping in to see Mr. Herbert with a score under his arm that turned out to be gorgeously bound in Morocco leather with beautiful gold-embossed letters on the cover that read "Mass in F, Dedicated to Victor Herbert."

Well, this odd character turned out to be a very wealthy amateur composer who had spent quite a few years getting this "Mass" down on paper.

It was still about forty-five minutes before curtain time, so Mr. Herbert took the score, settled back in his chair, and proceeded to look through the music, painstakingly scrutinizing every note on every page, while the small Donald Meek-Roland Young type chewed off his nails and perspired all over his necktie.

A half-hour later Victor Herbert closed the "Mass in F" and handed it back to his admirer and, fixing him with a curiously intense look, he said, "By God, it *is* in F!"

There was certainly nothing sadistic about Victor Herbert, but in every situation he wanted to be the one to supply the punch line. At one of the rehearsals a very fine violinist, of whose ability Mr. Herbert was fully aware, started to tiptoe out of the pit five minutes before the end of the session. Herbert stopped the orchestra and said, "Where are you going?" And the violinist said, "Excuse me, Mr. Herbert, I didn't think you'd mind my leaving a few minutes early. I have an appointment with a pupil to give a lesson."

Mr. Herbert said, "That's perfectly all right," and then he added, "Wouldn't hurt you to take one at the same time."

George Jessel will probably go down in show business history as the top master of ceremonies of all time, but if he has any competition, when the returns are all in, it will probably come from Chauncey Depew, who once wrapped up a chore at a certain Victor Herbert dinner that was as inspired a masterpiece of lifesaver emcee-ing as you'll ever run across in your whole born days.

It seems that a lot of Victor's well-meaning and slightly stuffy friends began gnawing at him to compose something more serious than musical comedy. "Victor," they would say, sort of like this, "your light little melodies, 'Kiss Me Again,' 'Thine Alone,' and so on, are all very well, but you were destined to be America's greatest composer, not just a tune writer, and it's time you were writing something important, like for instance the Great American Opera." After a certain length of time you can get so you believe even your own publicity, and before long Victor fell for all that nagging and started composing a grand opera.

Now every actor, composer, singer, writer, and comedian knows from sad experience that American Indian stuff can be neither tuneful, profound, moving, nor funny so far as the stage is concerned. When you put on a necklace of bear claws and a headdress of feathers and go jumping around on one foot, saying, "Ugh! How! Me wantum wampum," you are going to lay a big egg, and when you go around playing, "Moo-oon, moo-oon," on a floo-oot, you are not going to stir anybody's insides except that nice old lady from Sheboygan, Wisconsin, who stirs easy. Victor Herbert certainly knew that Indian stuff was dynamite, but by this time he was so drenched in hooey from so many sleeve-tuggers that he plunged headfirst into an Indian subject for his American grand opera and after a great many heartbreaking months he came up with a thing called *Natoma*.

I imagine that after Hannibal crossed the Alps and went back to his home town the local Rotarians planned a royal welcome that must have been a dilly, and I've heard that Lindbergh was rather well received at Le Bourget when he flew to Paris —but I'm sure that no one in history was ever received more enthusiastically than Victor Herbert was when he walked into the orchestra pit at the opera house for the première of his American grand opera *Natoma*. Oh, the lucky, lucky few thousands who were able to beg, steal, or forge tickets to the Metropolitan on that gala night! And of course the plans for the reception after the undoubted triumph included every kind of caviar, pheasant, and dignitary under glass that could possibly be squeezed into the banquet room at the Friars Club on West Forty-eighth Street. The only thing that nobody reckoned with was that this Indian grand opera might turn out to be probably the biggest flop of all time.

The disaster became apparent early in the first

act, and by the intermission all the people who were to attend the reception after the performance were clutching at their bosoms in agony, knowing they couldn't possibly go to this reception, and also knowing that they couldn't possibly *not* go. The critics left after the second act—which is customary on a lot of opening nights in New York so that the reviews can make tomorrow morning's papers, which are usually being sold in the streets as you come out of the theater.

The opera got worse clear down to the last curtain, which finally fell, like the hopes of the customers praying for a last-minute miracle. Off to the guillotine and the rack went some four hundred of New York's biggest celebrities to squirm and gulp and push the mushrooms around in the au jus and the lettuce around in the vinaigrette and their hearts around in their shoes and in their mouths, dreading the moment when the toastmaster would have to hit the crystal with the sterling and start the speeches. What could he say? What could *anybody* say?

The moment did come, and Chauncey Depew rose to his feet, and this is approximately what he said:

"Ladies and gentlemen, we are gathered here to pay tribute to our beloved Victor Herbert on the occasion of the première of his opera *Natoma*.

I think it would be appropriate at this time"—and he dug some clippings out of his pocket—"to read these reviews. The first one says, 'What happened last night in the opera house was neither opera nor drama. It certainly was not related to music in any way.' " By now the guests were ready to be carried out, and everybody thought the strain had been too much for Mr. Depew and that he had no doubt blown his cork. Everybody froze in his chair as Mr. Depew blandly continued reading reviews. "This one says, 'The performance last night at the opera was disgraceful—and should never have been allowed.' This one says, 'The composer of the new opera, the première of which we were unlucky enough to attend, may have talent for some things, but writing opera is quite obviously not one of them.' " After two more like that, Mr. Depew finally put the clippings back in his pocket and, looking out into the staring eyes of his horrified audience, he said, "Ladies and gentlemen, shortly before we sat down to this banquet I visited the library here in the Friars Club and collected the clippings I have just read to you. They were the actual reviews of the first performance of Bizet's opera Carmen." It would have taken the great Manitou himself to have saved Natoma, but Chauncey Depew's magic worked a miracle almost as great in saving Victor's face that fateful night.

However, there was no doubt about who supplied the punch line the time Mr. Herbert made a lunch date with a very fine conductor named Vic Baravelli. The idea of this lunch was that Herbert's new operetta was getting close to production and he wanted to discuss the orchestra with Mr. Baravelli, who was to conduct.

The lunch was as usual set for the Friars Club, and the conductor was waiting in the lobby, wondering what was holding up the "old man" on account of he was usually very punctual.

To kill time, Mr. Baravelli went over to glance at the bulletin board and saw a "flowers" list for some recently deceased member. He signed his name automatically, and then looked up at the top of the paper to see who it was that had passed on. The name was Victor Herbert.

$\mathcal{8}.$ AT THE RIALTO WE WORE GREEN VELVET
coats and starched white vests (laundry problems
again!), and if we were one minute late we missed
the whole overture because the orchestra pit was
an elevator, and when it went up, it went up, and
you couldn't sneak in till the lights went down
for the newsreel.

In my dreams, when I'm not skipping down
the steps of the old Mason City High School,
I'm usually standing with my heart in my mouth
on the Fiftieth Street subway platform, peering
up the tracks in the darkness, praying, praying,
PRAYING for a Broadway local so I wouldn't
miss that theater pit elevator.

They called me Down-beat Willson in those
days, also Wasp-waist Willson. I was pretty thin.

Hugo Riesenfeld was the conductor at the
Rialto. There was never anything like him in
Mason City. He was a real important figure on
Broadway and had a fur collar, a gold-headed cane,

a Homburg hat, and a Viennese accent. He had the most dramatic way of cuing the cymbal player, like he was reaching out fencing, or trying to spear a doughnut out of thin air, with his left hand stretched out in the opposite direction, pointing down to the floor like for balance. Everybody called him Doctor and he went to Europe every summer.

Meanwhile I had become a composer. I'd been writing all kinds of musical junk ever since I was old enough to hold a pencil, but now I'd finally gotten one thing published. A man isn't really a composer till this happens, and although I've never made a hole in one, I think it is entirely safe to say that there is no feeling like the one a person gets the first time he sees his own composition in print, *real print*. He is now a composer, his music is available to everybody, he has actually created something.

This happy event occurred because Dr. Riesenfeld had a secretary about my age whose name was Abe Meyer and still is. This Abe Meyer became my best friend and he pestered Dr. Riesenfeld and pestered him till he listened to one of my compositions called "Parade Fantastique." Between Abe and the Doctor they got it published for me, though it was quite a struggle, because I was pretty stubborn about making the necessary changes.

There's nothing more characteristic of human

nature than the peculiar illusion that our children can do no wrong. Let the neighbor's dog utter one plaintive little bleat at nine o'clock in the morning and you storm up and down about "that stupid, noisy mutt keeping me up half the night with his howling and yowling." But let your cat claw the sofa till it looks like shredded wheat with legs and you say, "Isn't she *smart!*"

This is why it is a very good plan whenever you write a new song or poem or book or whateveritis to put such a brain child away for a while till you can look at it a little more as though it were somebody else's brat instead of your own angel child.

Proud parenthood will fool the most discriminating creator. Ever hear Ellery Queen on the radio or read his books? Now you *know* there's nothing any more revoltingly corny than the way Sergeant Veelie calls Ellery "Maestro" every other speech—unless it's the way Sam Spade calls every crime a "caper"—yet the author clings to that little device of his as though he had made his great success entirely because of it instead of in spite of it.

And the funnies—whoever heard of anybody in this day and age saying "Hark!" But the fella who invented Little Orphan Annie apparently thinks that's real original dialogue. Let other people use old-fashioned talk like "What was that?" or "Listen!" No, Annie is gonna be different and keep right on saying "Hark!" till those little round pupil-less circles of hers are closed for good. In fact, I get so mad at her sometimes I'd like to be the one to do it.

And how about the fierce belief that the creator of Bathless Groggins has in that broken-down "Keerect!" that every character in his strip says day after day, year after year. I'm sure this artist is serenely positive that the day will come when Americans will quit saying things like "Okay" and "All right" and take on "Keerect" as a permanent part of the American language.

Anyway, Dr. Riesenfeld screamed at me about some mistakes in the form of my "Parade Fantastique" that I might have seen myself if I'd at least waited for the ink to dry before rushing it down to him as though it were a new fugue by Bach. If I'd happened to have taken it directly to a publisher I would probably have been laughed out of the building, and the great Cloud Twelve lift I got from having a published work might have been rather indefinitely postponed.

Dr. Riesenfeld has gone to his reward and Abe Meyer has been my good friend for twenty-five years and has given me more good advice than Damon ever gave Pythias or vice versa. Abe doesn't really come in until later, though.

Meanwhile, it is 1923 and Dr. Riesenfeld had been encouraging a man who had some ideas about making talking pictures. Dr. Riesenfeld was very remarkable because he was always interested in the other fellow's doings, so he paid me to go with my flute to this man's studio every morning at eight o'clock and play scales.

His place was the old Norma Talmadge Studio over on East Twenty-eighth Street, and I would play scales on my flute hour after hour while this man would record on film. The next day he would play it back and we would listen. There was so much surface noise and static scratching that you couldn't recognize the sound for a flute, but at least you knew you were hearing tones and the pitch was accurate.

Well, I never knew anyone to have the patience this man had. We would listen to yesterday's scales, and that night he would tear out every bit of insulation and rewire the whole studio— then in the morning more scales.

The next day we'd listen to the playbacks again, and sometimes the rewiring made it sound worse and sometimes slightly better. But either way, that patient man panned out little grains of golden know-how, and after a few months the scales not only played back as clear as could be, but now you knew it was a flute.

So Dr. Riesenfeld sent this man a few more players from his orchestra and we started playing pieces instead of scales, and the whole painstaking experiment started all over again. But pretty soon we were ready for the final test, which was to make a moving picture of a girl dancing and photograph the girl and record the music she was dancing to simultaneously on the same film.

Well, the music was Brahms's "A-Major Waltz," and if we played it once we played it ten thousand times, and to this day I can never hear it played without immediately seeing in front of me that small studio lighted in Boris Karloff green with that girl dancing, dancing, dancing day after day to the music of our four-piece orchestra huddled to the left of the camera, and back in the shadow, the calm, patient, kindly face of this man I've been telling you about—the Magnificent Failure, Dr. Lee De Forest.

That's what the *Saturday Evening Post* called him in a wonderful article. "Failure" only because everybody else but he got rich on his genius. "Magnificent" for obvious reasons. He is, as everybody knows, considered the father of radio and the talking picture. But I wonder sometimes if he's ever embarrassed at some of radio's jingle commercials, not to mention a couple of movies I've seen lately.

9. WELL, AFTER SOUSA AND THE RIALTO, I joined that obstinate, stubborn, spoiled, conceited, pampered, gorgeous instrument known as the Philharmonic Symphony Society of New York, being conducted in those years by Willem van Hoogstraten, Willem Mengelberg, and Wilhelm Furtwaengler.

I had joined this great orchestra as second flute, but one week before I was to begin this new job, John Amans, the first flute, got appendicitis and went to Europe to recuperate, so I ended up hearing the first symphony concert I'd ever gone to (not counting the matinee the Minneapolis Symphony once played in Mason City High School, to break the jump to Des Moines) from the chair of the first flute.

Anyhow, the first number the Philharmonic played that night was Beethoven's "Leonore," which we had rushed through rather sketchily at the rehearsal on account of everybody (but me) had played it a million times. At the concert I was a dude in a canoe shooting the rapids for the first time, jagged rocks every place right under the boat, but because I didn't know they were there I just leaned back and enjoyed it.

At the end of the overture the orchestra applauded and Van Hoogstraten, the conductor, rattled his baton against his stand. He was smiling and gesturing somewhere back of me, I thought, so I started to applaud, too, and looked around to see what I was missing.

The world's greatest piccolo player, Ernie Wagner, who sat next to me, said, "Get up and bow—whatsamatterwithyou?"

I did—as nonchalantly as possible—and early the next morning rushed over to ask my teacher, Mr. Barrère, if they always did that to a new member.

"What overture was it?" he said, and I said, " 'Leonore' by Beethoven."

Well, he started to laugh and rocked back and forth so furiously that his favorite chair, with him in it, turned a complete somersault and ended up upside down in the corner, his famous Parisian beard waving helplessly at the ceiling. He finally managed to say, "That overture has in it one of the most celebrated flute solos in the whole symphonic repertoire."

I helped the world's greatest flutist to his feet and his little boy, Jean, who was four years old by now, laughed and laughed, too, and for the first time I wasn't scared to death of my teacher.

"Mr. Barrère," I said, "how come you sort of seemed to expect me that first day I walked into your apartment and you were so especially nice to me, helping me get a job and all?"

He took a letter out of his desk which my mother had written him the day I left Mason City several years back, a typical mother's letter— "Take care of my boy, please. Help him to meet good people." You know, all those things a mother would write. Then I got good and scared all over again that Mr. Barrère might have figured that Mama was butting in and I was embarrassed and why are kids so dumb at that age?

Most people are scared an awful lot of the time —scared of any kind of change, scared of meeting new people, scared of the boss, scared of head-waiters—and when you look at somebody success-ful you say to yourself, "*He's* not scared of meet-ing new people and new things and the boss. That's probably why he's a success." Then one day you discover that he is scared, all right, but only manages to fool people into thinking he's not.

"Hey," you say to yourself, "this is a very im-portant secret about how to be a success." But the funny part is, you keep right on being scared of new people and changes and the boss, only pretending you're not and isn't that too bad?

Looking back to school days, how scared we used to be of the teacher. We know *now* that she was just as scared of us, maybe worse, and if we could just get that through our thick skulls we'd live longer and happier.

I honestly believe my life span has been considerably shortened because of silly suffering on a couple of occasions for no reason except being scared of people. The worst of all was once in the old high school building.

Funny how everything about that building sticks in my memory just as though it had happened this morning. I spent just as long in the new high school building, but those years are not sharp at all; in fact, hazy and fading. But that magnificent romantic symbol of worldliness and swaggering manhood, that sophisticated gray stone two-story wonderland, the old original Mason City High School . . . Mr. Beatty, full of a frightening authority, sweeping the echoy, tile-floored vestibule after school. Even that long-handled soft black-bristled broom was very special, different from any other broom. It went chunk-chunk into the corners, past the double doors of Mr. Hjort's physics laboratory. It slid elegantly down the steps from the assembly room, second floor, to the gymnasium in the basement—the steps I still skip down, four or five at a time, in my dreams. They were quite dignified steps, though, weren't they?

—only about three, four inches high, with thin rubber matting that made us thud to classes like we were all wearing tennis shoes.

I wonder why I remember the wire grille in the gymnasium door and windows, and Mr. Lines's big gold watch with the black fob that he always pulled out of his pocket at the beginning of algebra class. My gosh—I suddenly seem to remember a gold football hanging on that fob, and him so skinny and wearing glasses and all. I hope some of the kids asked him about that football. Imagine laying that watch out there on his desk in plain sight, day after day, and here it's taken me over thirty years to tumble to that little gold award he was so proud of. Could anything or anybody be more selfish and self-centered than high school kids? I'm sorry, Mr. Lines, I'm really sorry.

It's strange that I can still hear the exact pitch of my high school locker door as I slammed it shut, when I've long since forgotten the sound or appearance of my Carnegie Hall locker which I visited two, three times a day for the five years I was with the Philharmonic.

What is it people say about certain years being the impressionable ones?

Mr. Hammit was the principal, and his middle finger stayed bent at the joint. You could see it when he took a piece of chalk to write on the blackboard, which happens me to think of the hollow sound a nice new long piece of chalk made as you dropped it back into the wooden box with the little thumb piece to slide the top open with. Where did they keep that red and green chalk that appeared only for decorating the blackboard on Christmas?

Max Egloff asked me one day to join the B.D.C., the Boys Debating Club. He said they were having the annual dinner up at the high school that night, and me being musical and all, would I come and run the victrola from the sidelines, as it were, and at the same time see what a desirable club it was for me to join?

I went, and that was one experience that I'm sure cut my life expectancy down to an even three-score.

The dinner was held in the vestibule, known on such occasions as the Great Hall. There was the banquet table right in the middle, and over at the side by the drinking fountain, as naked as a cornet solo, was the victrola. No chair, no table, no records, no nuthin'. Someone forgot all about getting any records.

Everybody was all paired off, sitting at the long table, and there I was in my blue serge knickerbockers standing by the drinking fountain. Why didn't I just say, "Max asked me over to help out with the music, but there aren't any records, so good night, all"?

I don't know why, except that I was scared of people and felt so miserably conspicuous standing there in that hall with no records to play, trying to blend into the wall and escape from what was now a reverberating, horrifying, cubistic nightmare—not belonging to the club and all, and with no exit line.

After a half-hour of being bound to this exquisitely refined torture wheel, the president of the club crooked his finger at me and I walked barefooted over the treadmill course of broken glass, spikes, and burning coals that lay between my wall and his seat in the president's chair.

He handed me a note and whispered for me to take it around to Max Egloff, who was sitting down at the foot of the table. I got back onto another endless belt of fire and spikes and delivered the note.

You know, my face is burning up right now just thinking of it. I was sure, of course, that the note said, "Get rid of this idiot," because Max handed me a quarter and said, "Thanks for coming over. Good night."

A tip yet.

Well, how I got from that table out into God's wonderful cool outdoors was the one thing about my high school days that was a complete double exposure, and the funny thing was that when Max handed me the twenty-five cents he accidentally gave me the note, too, and when I got home I read it just before turning on the gas. What the note actually said was: "This fella must think we're nuts forgetting those records. Now he'll never join the club. If you're flush enough, treat him to a picture show. I'll split it with you later."

Being scared like that is all vanity, I guess—scared we won't make a hit with people. I was hired one time to play my first record date down at the Columbia Studios on Fourteenth Street. Robert Hood Bowers, who wrote *East Is West*, was the conductor, but even though I was already in the New York Philharmonic this was all new and I was scared of him and I didn't know any of the other musicians, so I was scared of them. No reason—just because everything and everyone was new and a change from my own particular little rat race where I felt at home.

I put my flute together, sat down, and the date began. About halfway through, the man next to me started singing to himself, "Standing on the outside, looking on the inside."

Well, I lost another five years off my life right then. I felt sure he meant I was an outsider and that he was making fun of me because I had never played a record date before, and of course I suffered like a condemned soul the rest of the afternoon.

After the date he came up, very embarrassed,

and introduced himself and said, "Never played with one of you Philharmonic men before. How did I do?"

The blood rushed back into my body and I complimented him on his playing and he thanked me and walked away, whistling a very popular tune of the day which I would have known if I hadn't been such a long-hair: "Standing on the outside, looking on the inside, waiting for the evening mail."

I think most people are that way—scared of things—and about all we can do is try our best not to act scared and give as good a performance as possible. You can always find somebody scareder, you know.

Kreisler used to have to put powder on his fingers when he played the fiddle on account of he perspired so from being scared, and all the time he was acknowledged the world's greatest.

When you play in an orchestra you're scared of the conductor, and when you become a conductor you're scared of the orchestra because they're the ones who can really tell whether you know your stuff or not.

Mengelberg, the Philharmonic's famous Dutch conductor, who followed Van Hoogstraten, was a bogeyman to me—for a special reason. The superplush soft green promenade on the left side of Carnegie Hall used to be the locker room and there was one Carnegie Hall locker in there that I *do* remember. I'm speaking of Teddy Cella's locker. He was the solo harpist of the New York Philharmonic. Still is. He was the Beau Brummel of the orchestra, so he had a mirror hanging on the inside of his locker, and one day I was standing over by it telling Teddy and a few more the joke about the musician in the insane asylum who had played with all the great conductors, and this musician was perfectly normal till you mentioned Mengelberg. Then he suddenly became a writhing, quivering, screaming mass of idiocy.

As I got to the climax of this joke and started rolling hysterically on the floor, I seemed to feel that my audience was gripped in an oddish kind of fascination, which caused me to enlarge upon my lunacy performance to unusually inspired lengths.

I was confident I had given a socko portrayal, all right, so I was pretty dumfounded when I got no laughs at all. In fact, as I stumbled to my feet I realized I had laid a spectacular egg. I found out why, though, as soon as I got a glimpse in Teddy's mirror of the very unsmiling face of one member of that fascinated audience I hadn't noticed because he was standing behind me. Sure, it was Mengelberg.

I stayed awake for weeks shuddering over that boner. But no matter how big a boner you pull, someone has pulled a worse one and lived through it. It is very wise, even sage, to keep somebody else's colossal blunders in mind at all times so that when you do some horrible, stupid thing you can remember that somebody else was even stupider once and you may gain considerable comfort thereby.

I am indebted to Cecil B. DeMille for the boner I carry around in my mind, which is double assurance on account of Mr. DeMille is such a successful fellow—real important and all.

It was the first wartime dinner of the Academy of Motion Picture Arts and Sciences only a few weeks after Pearl Harbor. Willkie spoke, then the Chinese Ambassador, and then in the clean-up position Cecil B. DeMille arose. Mr. DeMille said, "I was greatly impressed with Mr. Willkie's remarks and thrilled at the words of the celebrated speaker who followed him—the *Japanese* Ambassador."

Now you see you can never be in a much more embarrassing position than that. And nobody held it against Mr. DeMille and he got over it all right, and here, not so many years later, it's not a catastrophe at all, only an anecdote, and isn't that nice to know?

10. I CAN THINK OF THREE THINGS THAT
don't taste as good as they smell: (1) coffee being
ground in that big old red grocery-store grinder,
(2) that toasty cigarette smell when you get your
light from the dashboard lighter, and (3) gasoline.
Now I don't drink gasoline, but instinctively I
know it doesn't taste as good as it smells.

When I drive up to the gas station and the attendant says, "You need some oil," I say, "Okay."
And then he says, "What do you use—about
thirty?" I always stare thoughtfully off into space
for a moment or two and then I say, "Yeah—yeah
—thirty'll be all right." You know, I have absolutely no idea what that "thirty" means?

After going to filling stations for a quarter of a
century, it was only last week that an attendant
told me how I could remember which side my
tank is on—it's on the same side as the steering
wheel. And it isn't as though I haven't given the
boys a chance to tell me, because it's an Iowa
trait to enjoy a visit here and there. Not that we

Iowans are what you would say garrulous—merely thorough. A mite stubborn, perhaps, along with it, but any running-off-at-the-mouth we may do is simply our natural conscientiousness with respect to detail. In fact, it is just as characteristic for an Iowan to clam up, as you might say, particularly when the circumstances pród at his native contrariness.

I was driving along the Iowa side of the Mississippi down near Dubuque one time and happened to see a homemade sign leaning against a nice fat-looking red barn, with a redheaded farmer doing likewise against the sign.

It read: "Fresh Smoked Sturgeon for Sale," which is a great, great delicacy, so I stopped full of enthusiasm and said, "Like to get some sturgeon."

The farmer moved his head one sixteenth of an inch and said, "They're yonder." I looked yonder, not to say hither and thither, but couldn't see any fish anyplace, so I said, "Well—uh—could you pick me out a couple pounds?"

This time he never moved at all, never even blinked, and with the timothy still in the corner of his mouth he said, "Hain't no pick to 'em. They're all about the same."

Papa was a bit on the stubborn side. He had Scotch-English forebears, he was redheaded, and he was born in Iowa. Brother, that's stubborn. To the day he died he insisted on calling his favorite movie actress "An-eye-ta" Stewart. I told him Miss Stewart called herself Aneeta, but his hair merely turned a shade redder and he said, "She's mistaken."

Papa went to Notre Dame and learned to pitch curves from baseball's first curve pitcher, fellow named Candy Cummings. One year Notre Dame played an exhibition game with the Chicago White Sox and Papa lost the game but got a medal for pitching seventeen strike-outs. The reason he was so hot while his teammates were so cold was because he had a girl from the Armour Institute sitting out in far center field under an apple tree, with her lace mitts and pink parasol, and Papa was anxious to get each inning over with as fast as possible so he could get on back to the apple tree and make time with this nice young lady. He did, too, I guess, because I am their son.

Papa also played the E-flat cornet in the Notre Dame band but gave it up for the guitar as he mellowed into middle age. His specialty was the "Spanish Fandango." For people who could only play a few chords, someone had invented a clamp to put on the neck of the instrument, which raised the key as you clamped the device higher on the neck, making a pretty accomplished-sounding guitar player out of a pretty ordinary strummer. The name for this clamp is a very fancy Italian phrase, *capo d'astro*, which I didn't find out till I got into the Philharmonic because the closest Papa could come to saying it in Iowa talk was "cabadaster." They still call it that back home. Mama's family played the guitar too—her brother, Uncle Olin, and all her sisters—Aunt Lida, Aunt Belle, and Aunt June, and also Gramma Reiniger.

Gramma was not Scotch-English, redheaded, nor Iowan, but she could give Papa cards and spades when it came to being stubborn. She was ninety-four years old and was dying. The doctor had for several weeks been feeding her, to her great disgust, on lukewarm broth and thin stuff like diluted junket and weak tea.

One day a truck farmer named Mr. Skudder stopped by on his monthly visit from his truck farm with home-bottled pickles and ketchup and triple-strength horse-radish guaranteed to grow hair on a china egg. He gave a loud pull on the front-door bell and everybody rushed shushing and whispering to quiet him. Gramma opened her eyes and said, "Who's that?" And when Aunt Lida said, "Only Mr. Skudder with his horse-radish," Gramma said, "Get him in here with a bottle of it and a tablespoon." She opened the bottle herself and poured out a heaping spoonful, which she immediately polished off. Then she smacked her lips and glared at the doctor and spoke her last words on this earth, "Now there's something with a little character!"

11. THE NEW YORK PHILHARMONIC ORCHES-
tra made a spring tour every year that ended with
a matinee in Pittsburgh. After the matinee Fritz
Geib, the tuba player, used to go down to Dim-
ling's Restaurant and bring back a lot of "lunch,"
he used to call it, for the train on the way back to
New York. Mr. Geib's greatest pleasure in life
was fixing "lunch" for the entire Philharmonic
every year on the way home from the Pittsburgh
matinee.

The train left around 9 P.M., and Mr. Geib
would take over the smoking room and lay out
rye bread, salami, liverwurst, Swiss cheese, baloney,
dill pickles, and tubs of beer.

Mr. van Praag was the orchestra manager, and
he was real kind and friendly and always tried to
make a new member feel easy and not strange.

On the train one evening Mengelberg was, as
usual, making like Beethoven in his double Pullman seat. He was a pretty good hypochondriac

when it came to catching cold, and he used to sit in the train with practically his whole wardrobe on him—two sweaters and suit coat, several scarves and fur overcoat, a yarn toboggan cap, and a big fur shako on top of that.

He sure looked overstuffed, and this particular night he was also looking very jolly and red-faced, as he was feeling unusually expansive and regal. In spite of prohibition, he always had some special luggage full of his favorite European beverages which he was allowed to bring in to America each year through some kind of diplomatic immunity he was said to enjoy.

To an Iowa boy like me, all that drinking was to be frowned on; nevertheless, there was a vicarious fascination in such man-of-the-world activity as was going on back in the royal end of that Pullman, and I couldn't resist hanging around the edge of the fringe of the chosen few—only first-chair men, of course—who were laughing at Mengelberg's Dutch anecdotes between sips of his Bols gin, a delectable stimulant that came in an earthenware crock and which he passed around with a great show of generosity. Mr. van Praag spotted me in the group and said something to Mengelberg in Dutch. Mengelberg looked at me and his red face broke into a toothy laugh as he answered, also in Dutch; but my high school German came in real handy and I was able to break down the guttural "boppum, hoppum, gebloppum" Hollander sounds into the following dialogue:

Mr. van Praag: "Maestro, how about passing a drink to the new young American flute player?"

Mengelberg: "What! Are you crazy! Asking me to waste good Holland gin on the second flute!"

Just about that time the Pullman conductor started to sing "In the Evening by the Moonlight," and being an old quartet man, I naturally jumped in on the tenor part. Well, it was no good as a duet, so I started to hunt up a bass and a baritone.

Now on this train were one hundred and five of the world's finest orchestral musicians, and I couldn't find one man who could fake a little barbershop harmony—not one. We ended up as a trio—me, the Pullman conductor, and Jimmy Carrol, the orchestra's baggageman!

It's a good thing I could fake back home in Mason City when I played in the high school band because, if you stop to think for a moment, the flute and piccolo are the only instruments that you *don't* hold in front of you, so when you're playing in a marching band there's no possible way you can hook your music onto your instrument or anyplace else and still see it.

The trombones have a lead-pipe cinch. Their lyres hook onto the bell of their instruments right in front of them. The same with the trumpets and clarinets. You may think a lyre is a Greek lute, but it is also a music holder. Even the bass drum player has a lyre that fits on the tightening clamps of his instrument. But lo, the poor piccolo player!

Submarines, flying boats, robots, talking pictures, radio, television, bouncing radar vibrations off the moon, rocket ships, and atom-splitting—all in our time. But nobody has yet been able to figure out a music holder for a marching piccolo player.

Just for the record, Mr. Bushgens, who owned the harness shop in Mason City, made some very interesting experiments in this direction back in 1915. Mr. Bushgens was going to do this or know why. You may know that Mr. Bushgens was a man of considerable imagination when I tell you that his son's name was Merlin—the only Merlin I ever knew outside the Knights of the Round Table.

Well, Mr. Bushgens's first attempt was the chest lyre. This was an elaborate breastplate affair that tied in the back with several laces. Not what you would call a "one-man top," exactly, but my brother Cedric was only too glad to lace me into it. And swooping out from the breastplate came a curved arm, and on this arm was soldered the lyre to hold the music.

The day Mr. Bushgens finished this magnificent harness was a proud one for us both. Cedric strapped it on me and I rushed off to rehearsal.

"It won't bob up and down like this when I'm only marching instead of running," I said to myself, but I was sure wrong. It bobbed the music right out of the lyre before we hit the trio of the first march.

Mr. Bushgens was down but not out. He immediately abandoned the first idea and started to concentrate on the left biceps which, in case none of you play the piccolo, automatically swings around to the front as you raise the instrument to your lips. Mr. Bushgens's plan was simply to attach an upright lyre to a wide leather strap which would buckle around my upper arm. This time I didn't get halfway to the trio before the circulation was completely shut off and my left arm and fingers became entirely useless.

So, as I started to say, it was a very good thing I knew how to fake. My only difficulty was that I could never remember which marches finished on the down beat, like "Semper Fidelis," and which ones had that extra "bump" on the end which we call the "button" in the music business. So the most noticeable thing about the Mason City High School band during the years I was there was the florid piccolo obbligato that seemed to be a characteristic of every piece this band played, not to mention the frequent apologetic little "ploop" at the end after everyone else had finished.

I was beginning to have youthful theories about

GIRLS around this time when I wasn't playing the piccolo. One of these theories was that a boy and a girl who had never met could, merely by looking at each other, establish a romantic contact sufficiently fraught with stuff to end in a kiss without one spoken word having passed between them. This theory occurred to me some years later in the Philharmonic when, after the Pittsburgh matinee one season, I got down to the station about a half-hour early and was hanging around the waiting room, waiting for the New York train and Mr. Geib's cold "lunch."

It certainly wasn't a flirtation, but I became aware of a swell-looking little dish sitting on one of the benches. My "theory" flashed into my head and I began to wonder if this was the time to try it out.

We looked at each other for the better part of the half-hour, and just as I realized it was time to get aboard, she started out toward the train. Right next to the New York track was a local suburban job that she was apparently heading for. She got on and sat in the corner seat where the candy butcher usually is.

We looked at each other through the glass and I said to myself, "Now or never." Both trains started to move. I jumped on the local and went just inside the door to her seat. She looked up at me, not at all surprised, and I bent down and kissed her. We smiled at each other and I jumped off and barely caught the rear end of my train's observation car just as her window flashed past.

Neither of us had spoken a word and we never saw each other again, and I only brought up this story because I thought that that girl might possibly read it here someday and—— Oh, never mind.

12. MR. MENGELBERG, AS I HAVE SAID somewhere before, was at this time the conductor of the Philharmonic. One of his most annoying characteristics was a habit of putting special signs in all the music. Considering the many times we had played Tschaikowsky's "Fifth Symphony," the famous horn solo was marked up so badly you couldn't see the notes any more. There was a crescendo or diminuendo of ff or pp or something marked over, above, around, or beside every single note on the page.

Mr. Jaenicke, the horn player, was a very patient man, but just before the rehearsal began one morning he went to Mengelberg. "Mr. Mengelberg, I bought a new horn part for the Tschaikowsky 'Fifth Symphony' which I have here in my hand because I cannot read the other part any more because I can't see the notes for the marks. Would you be good enough to put on this clean part exactly the expression marks you would like me to observe?"

Mr. Mengelberg said, "You haff ze old part?" Mr. Jaenicke handed him the old part. After studying it for a few moments Mr. Mengelberg said, "Zis old part is pairfectly fine, except you must can add a crescendo here and a diminooendo at zis blace, one more forte in ze next measure, and two more pianissimos by ze end."

When I first joined the Philharmonic there were two symphonies in New York, the Philharmonic and the Damrosch orchestra. The Philharmonic boys felt, of course, very superior to the Damrosch gang, and vice versa. Some years before, these rivals of ours started a story about a venerable old gentleman named Stransky who had conducted the Philharmonic early in the century. The story was about Stransky having a dream that he was strapped in the electric chair. The warden came in and released him, saying, "It's no use, boys. Don't you know Stransky is a non-conductor?"

As reprisal, any little insights into the penurious side of Dr. Walter Damrosch were whispered into existence and started on their rounds, you may be sure, by the dear fun-loving lads of the Philharmonic.

It became, thus, generally known that this world-famous dean of conductors always left a five-cent tip in the Carnegie Hall restaurant. He was supposed to have extracted this gratuity from his person in somewhat the involved way that Jack Benny visits his sub-cellar vault on the radio, with a great fluttering of moths and clanking of chains. Also it was said that the rented limousine that brought Dr. Damrosch to the concerts did not collect him at his home but picked him up, top hat and all, at the Columbus Circle subway station only three blocks from Carnegie Hall. And unkindest of all, it became whispered behind fans that the blue denim rehearsal shirt this great American conductor invariably wore daily was not a different edition for each appearance but was always one and the same shirt. Of course the favorite story was to the effect that the famous Leopold Damrosch, father of Walter and Frank, was said to have remarked at some time during their youth, "The deepest regret of my life is that neither of my sons has evidenced any talent for music whatsoever."

It was also well known, particularly among the symphony musicians of the town, that you did not under any circumstances ever answer Dr. Damrosch back if he made a critical suggestion to you during rehearsal. Getting in an argument with that lightning intellect and rapier tongue was like backing south into a McCormick harvester going north. My flute teacher, Georges Barrère, who played with the Damrosch Symphony, obituaried a brace of tuts for a foolhardy colleague who attempted to parry a Damrosch thrust one hapless morning. After they had swept up the body Mr. Barrère said, "Poor fellow, he lost a great chance to shut up."

New York having two symphonies meant that the Philharmonic had to share Carnegie Hall with the Damrosch orchestra and take turns every other week rehearsing upstairs in the small hall that we called the "torture chamber" on account of it was an old-fashioned little chamber-music hall, built without any windows, to accommodate something like a string quartet and an audience of about seventy-five polite and restrained ladies-of-the-Wednesday-Music-Club members. It was a pretty miserable place for a hundred-piece symphony orchestra to rehearse in.

However, a log cabin sheltered the babe Lincoln, a humble cottage begat Shakespeare, and the torture chamber on the sixth floor of Carnegie Hall fathered the first giant sounds from at least one of the world's great masters that I know of. On this particular morning we were noodling and preluding in the listless manner that the prospect of a session in that ghastly hall always inspired. I opened my music, and the first number was the Tschaikowsky "B-Flat Piano Concerto."

"Who's the soloist today?" I asked John Amans, who sat next to me and who had just returned from Europe. And John said, "Only the world's greatest pianist," and he threw a comedy-sounding name at me.

"Kidding aside, John, who *is* the soloist?"

"I just told you," John said. "He's a new young player whose European concerts have killed all the people."

I turned to the fella behind me. "Sam, ever hear of this new guy?"

"No," he said.

I called over to the cellist in front of me. "Ennio, who's playing today?"

"Nobody much," he said. "Somebody mentioned his name, but I forget it."

I sneered loudly at John just as Mengelberg walked in to start the rehearsal. He was followed by an anemic high school sophomore in a pink shirt who looked like he was apologizing for being alive as he sat down nervously at the big concert grand, sniffling from a runny nose.

Mengelberg leaned back on his throne, took off his watch, crossed his little fat legs, ran his fingers through his mop, and said, "Szhentlemen, for ze first time in America I present you one of ze great pianists von our time." And when he mentioned the name practically nobody applauded, but a few boys laughed, a couple of fiddle players absently hit their bows on their stands, and I sneered once more at Mr. Amans.

The young man's nose was dripping very noticeably by now, but apparently he was used to it because he didn't pay any attention. Mengelberg glared around the room, hit the throne a couple of times with his stick, and finally threw the down beat.

Well, this pink boy crashed down onto the keyboard with the most electrifying sound I'd ever heard in my whole born days, and by the end of the first movement that two-by-four hall was rocking with the most majestic, monumental reverberations in the history of the building, mixed with the hysterical shouts of the dignified, superior gentlemen of the Philharmonic: Horowitz had played in Carnegie Hall for the first time.

13. FOR SOME REASON OR OTHER, A
"modern" trend raised its ugly, cacophonous
schnozola along about this time and nurtured a
considerable number of noisy neurotics who were
particularly active in chamber music. The sounds
that are now to be heard in a certain classy ten-
cent store on Forty-second Street, between Fifth
and Sixth avenues, are much more musical than
some of the Sunday-night orgies that went on at
that same location in the twenties, which was not
a ten-cent store in those days but a sedate stained-
glass-and-blond-wood little affair known as Aeolian
Hall.

Certain of those chamber-music concerts from
'24 to '29 would curl your hair, curdle your blood,
and convince you, once and for all, that music
with no melody and no beauty of harmony is just
ugly, smart-alecky, contrived noise that should
have no place in our solar system at all, let alone
in posterity's affectionate bosom. And I hope the

oblivion that has swallowed up the nerve-racking, junky, mathematical monkey business we had to perform in those days will forever remind some of the great composers who were guilty of that garbage never to confuse trigonometric orgasms with music again.

Any of you misguided survivors of those sandy, uninspired, sawdust, barren, barren days—any of you who are within sound of my voice—look back, please, on those miserably involved, cackling, cracking, bloodless monstrosities. Dig them out of their lonely sarcophagi just long enough to compare their termite-filled pages with some of the Respighi and Stravinsky and Gershwin miracles wrought in those same years, and then let your souls fill with remorse that you could have done so much accountless frittering.

The only one of those "masterpieces" I can remember was a twenty- or thirty-minute hunk of hideous sniveling called "The Rat and the Death." About halfway through this piece there was a lengthy and elaborate piccolo cadenza representing the rat, which was followed by the death-rattle motif played on an instrument invented by the composer, whose name we charitably omit. This instrument consisted of ten or twelve ginger-ale bottles filled to varying degrees with water and "played" with a xylophone mallet.

I was halfway through the cadenza when over my music stand I caught a glimpse of my teacher, Georges Barrère, sitting in the audience. His fastidiously elegant Parisian beard was vibrating. In fact, he was shaking all over on account of he was dying laughing inside and was trying his best not to show it. This struck me as pretty funny, and the farther I got into this idiotic solo, the closer I came to breaking up myself.

By this time I was spitting out any kind of note on the piccolo, anything to keep going. But presently I spluttered off into silence after gasping out a few last squeaks that aren't on anybody's piccolo.

As I was trying to sneak out the stage door after the concert, I ran into the writer of this so-called composition and he grasped my hand with fervent, ecstatic, grateful thank-you noises, saying that my performance of the piccolo cadenza was the most magnificent interpretation of anything he had ever heard in his life.

Way back as early as arithmetic and geography they taught me that we cannot improve on certain "positives"; stuff that is round or square or perfect, for instance, cannot be made rounder or squarer or perfecter. And while they were at it, they could have included the chromatic scale which, as you no doubt know, is Mr. Bach's principle whereby Mr. Steinway and Mr. Baldwin and the different ones arrange those black and white keys on the piano, exactly one half tone apart.

But wouldn't you know that somebody thought it would be even better to find some new notes "in the cracks," as you might say; and so back there in those frantic, futile twenties, various groups got to experimenting with one fourth, one sixteenth, and even one thirty-second tones, and one group called "The Thirteenth Sound Ensemble of Havana" got Columbia Phonograph to record a composition written for special instruments that could play those in-the-cracks notes. This piece is called "Cristobal Colon Prelude" and is very interesting as a novelty and collector's item. They overlooked one thing, however: when you tighten up a chromatic scale to the extent of putting a couple more notes *between* every white and black key on the piano, the net result, when you perform such a scale, is a sound that descends or ascends so smoothly that it's no longer music—it's a slide whistle, or a musical saw, or a fire siren, or a buzz saw on a busy day at the planing mill.

The greatness of a Beethoven or a da Vinci was in knowing when he was in the "done—finished— that's-all-there-is-there-isn't-any-more" department. One more note or one more flick of the brush would not make the passage or the painting better, it would make it worse, and it's kind of too bad that we don't recognize that in a lot of everyday things—the automobile, for instance. I can't see but what we might very well have left alone some of the big old comfortable thirty-mile-an-hour models and even the smooth, silent, elegant electrics with the ebony-and-gold steering handle. To what ends did we develop streamlined family cars that can go eighty or a hundred miles an hour? Who benefits by that? Who likes it? Maybe we have arrived at a point where we ought to think twice before cheerfully accepting the theory that if a scale with twelve half tones is good, a scale with twenty-four quarter tones must be twice as good, and one with forty-eight sixteenth tones would be out of this world.

14. AT THE END OF EVERY SEASON THE dear old Philharmonic was prostituted, as you might say, to the extent of giving several post-season concerts to any aspiring conductors who had the money to pay for them.

One of these has gone down to immortality not from the quality of his conducting, but for the classic remark he made to the orchestra as he started to rehearse the Beethoven "Fifth" with us: "Gentlemen—you know this piece and I know it, so please don't look at me. It makes me nervous."

Another ambitious time-beater—who was willing to lay it on the line so that he could include "guest conductor of the New York Philharmonic" on his stationery—came to us preceded by a rather curious reputation. It seemed that he always insisted on personally tuning each individual instrument in the whole orchestra before every concert.

"May I hear your A string, please?" he'd say. "Ah-ah-ah-ah, it's juuuuust a little sharp—that's better. There we are. Thenk yo veddy much. Next!"

Well, the gentlemen in the cello section decided to frame this human tuning fork, so before the concert, when all the cellos were lined up outside his dressing room, the first cellist in the section went in and presently came out all properly tuned to the conductor's satisfaction and then simply passed his instrument along to the next man, who went inside and dutifully readjusted the peg of his A string as directed. "Ah-ah-ah-ah, it's juuuuust a little sharp—that's better. There we are. Thenk yo veddy much. Next."

And all ten of the cellists carried the same cello back into the dressing room and soberly retuned it each time.

I was on the Philharmonic Orchestra Committee by this time, to meet with the Board of Directors once a year merely because in high school English was my very best subject and I made a noise like I was pretty smart. We were trying to get an additional five dollars a week per man for the summer season, and our ace in the hole was a viola player who greatly admired Bruckner, one of the master composers of the last century.

Now we are told that Bruckner, in spite of the great music he wrote, was very eccentric—didn't bother about bathing and wore a beard that collected things during the day: soup, coffee, tobacco. Our viola player had, as a sort of personal tribute to Bruckner, raised whiskers and he also ate chocolate most of the time because that collected noticeably in his beard and gave him a very Brucknerish look. We had him waiting outside the board room and told the directors—Mr. Clarence Mackay, Mr. Otto Kahn, Mr. Triller, and a couple others—that many of our members couldn't live on the prevailing wage. In fact, "one viola player is practically living on chocolate bars," we said. We opened the door, brought him in as "Exhibit A" with his beard full of Hersheys, and got the raise without a struggle.

Bruckner, as you may know, was the teacher of Mahler, and Mengelberg was about the only conductor in the country to perform Mahler's music. He used to ram it down the public's throat once or twice a season when he would program one of the interminable Mahler symphonies.

At the rehearsal he would always say to us, always, ALWAYS, in that incredible accent of his, "Szhentlemen—you must can like this moosic. Mahler iss ze Bateoffen von our time."

Not satisfied with his unique accent, Mengelberg used to invent words. "Tee-totto" meant crisply marked. "Tee-tottissimo" meant very crisply marked. Ševčík was a world-famous violinist especially renowned for his brilliant bowing, so

Mengelberg tried to coerce brilliant bowing from his string section by often asking for "Ševčík-issimo."

But one Mengelbergian expression had everybody stumped: "the Bismarck bow." In fact, nobody knew what he meant until years after he went back to Holland. By that time some genius had figured out that Bismarck was bald except for two or three hairs, so when Mengelberg asked for "the Bismarck," he was only trying to get the string players to play lightly, with—if possible—only two or three hairs of the bow.

15. FURTWAENGLER FINALLY GOT THE JOB away from Mengelberg, but he was soon getting the old fish eye from the Philharmonic's Board of Directors, who were thinking about trying to bring the one-and-only out of Italy—Toscanini.

The music critic on the *Herald Tribune*, Lawrence Gilman, had written Furtwaengler's epitaph in the nature of a scathing review of what most of us in the orchestra thought was a very magnificent all-Wagner concert, and Maestro Toscanini had now replaced Furtwaengler as the Philharmonic's permanent conductor.

Mr. Toscanini hates to have people tell stories about his unbelievable sense of hearing and his fabulous memory, both of which he insists are accidents that could happen to anybody. Musicianship is all that really matters, according to the Maestro. Be that as it may, I'm sure going to tell a story about the ears that can hear the grass grow, and if he ever reads it I hope he'll forgive me.

The great Italian composer, Respighi, wrote a new symphonic poem called "Feste Romane" and dedicated it to Toscanini, who naturally was to give the first performance. Came Monday-morning rehearsal and we were about to run through the new Respighi piece for the first time. The first movement describes children screaming their brains out at play on the streets of Rome and is scored—to make the highest, squeakiest, most unpleasant, unmusical racket you can imagine—for piccolos, high violins sawing away just under the bridge, and a little squealing E-flat clarinet squeaking out a high F sharp, while the rest of the orchestra, including four drummers, play practically anything they like.

We hit the down beat, which sounded like a boxcar full of Decker's Iowana Hams and Bacons with their tails caught in the wringer. Mr. Toscanini stopped the awful racket with a gesture and glared coldly at Mr. Gerhardt, the E-flat clarinet player. "F sharp, F sharp, F sharp," he said hoarsely (he says everything hoarsely).

We made a fresh start and the Maestro broke his nice long baton over the concertmaster's music stand. He doesn't use any music stand himself. He conducts everything from memory, even at rehearsals, so he doesn't need one. "F sharp, F sharp, *fa diesis, fa diesis, O Dio, vergogna, ver-*

gogna, in Italian means it's a shame, vergogna, F sharp, F sharp!"

When he's good and mad he translates as he goes along any insulting Italian words he might use to make sure you get the idea.

His voice got louder and wilder as he looked helplessly into the empty house crying out for F sharp.

Well, that went on for five or six starts. By this time Mr. van Praag, the orchestra manager, had rushed over to Mr. Gerhardt—who would have been far better pleased if he were dead—and was whispering, "Jacob, play F sharp, the Maestro says play F sharp."

Poor Mr. Gerhardt rolled his eyes and moaned, "I am playing F sharp. I've been playing it since the beginning."

Now I must interrupt myself at this point to ask you to observe the clarinetist next time you go to a concert. Sooner or later you will see him hold up his instrument horizontally and blow out water from under certain of the very small keys. This is almost a subconscious gesture and is done automatically every once in a while.

Mr. Gerhardt was so upset that without actually knowing what he was doing he picked up his little clarinet and blew on the keys. The Maestro raised his baton one last time and threw a sensational down beat at the orchestra. Out came the squealing, hideous, cacophonous sound for the ump-teenth time, and the Maestro sank weakly down in his chair, whispering, "At last F sharp—*grazie a Dio!*"

Mr. Gerhardt *had* been fingering F sharp all the time, but a little water under the key had caused it to sound F natural and the Maestro *heard* it through all that dissonance when the man who actually played the note didn't even hear it himself!

Two things Mr. Toscanini was always consistent about: (1) never play Tschaikowsky and (2) never have a soloist on any of his concerts excepting the Beethoven "Ninth."

I don't remember exactly when he broke Rule Number One about no Tschaikowsky, but I guess it's lucky he did, because Vladimir Horowitz became his son-in-law, and Mr. Horowitz, as everybody knows, is the best Tschaikowsky player in the business.

The Maestro broke Rule Number Two because he wanted very much to do an important American symphonic work, and thinking about this, he became impressed with Ernest Schelling's "Impressions from an Artist's Life," for piano and orchestra, so he invited Mr. Schelling to play this work with him.

Came Monday morning and we started to rehearse Mr. Schelling's piece. As a rule, when a soloist rehearses with a symphony orchestra, he leaves out the cadenza (an elaborate hunk of showing off in which the soloist is entirely on his own), as there is no sense in wasting time wading through this cadenza with the orchestra sitting there doing nothing at so much per hour. On this occasion, however, Mr. Schelling kept right on going when he hit the cadenza, and Mr. Toscanini didn't stop him but listened attentively.

Halfway through, the Maestro did stop him, though, and said, "Mr. Schelling, I believe you omitted the G flat from that last series of arpeggios you just played," and Mr. Schelling replied, "You are right. I did omit the G flat because I never wrote a G flat at that particular point in my original score."

"I do not wish to disagree, Mr. Schelling. After all, you wrote the work."

"That's right, Mr. Toscanini."

"However, if you will hand me the score, please, Mr. Guidi?"

The Maestro never hammed it up to the extent of leaving the score off the stage. Even though he never looked at it during rehearsals he always had it handy on a chair next to the concertmaster, Scipione Guidi.

Mr. Guidi handed up the score to the Maestro, who immediately thumbed his way over to the cadenza. Making no comment, he passed the score along to Mr. Schelling, who took a look, turned slightly pale, took another look, and stood up.

"Mr. Toscanini," he said, "I *did* omit the G flat. In all the times I have played this piece I *always* omitted the G flat. Since the day I wrote it I had completely forgotten there was one there."

The Maestro picked up his baton in that famous right-hand grip of his—he holds the stick somehow without bending his fingers—rested his left hand lightly on his hip, cocked his head ever so slightly in Mr. Schelling's direction, tossed us a down beat, and the rehearsal went on.

The next year the Maestro disappeared into the Astor Hotel as soon as he arrived from Italy and didn't come out all season. We didn't know whether he was sick or superstitious, on account of one day we heard he was sick and the next day we heard he was waiting for the right "vibrations" or the proper signs of the zodiac or whatever superstition it is that has been rumored to be pretty important to him.

The main thing was that nobody knew from day to day whether he would show up at Carnegie Hall or not, which made it a little tough on the management, not to mention the billboard paster who puts up the advance six-sheets around the outside of Carnegie Hall.

Anyway, I remember we went to the rehearsals all winter long, hoping to see the trim little patent-leather feet, the immaculate black silkish chin-high coat, the unbelievably neat mustache, the satin-smooth cheeks, and those dark, friendly, stormy, warm, frightening, nearsighted, far-seeing eyes. All we got, though, morning after morning, was a boring session with some frenzied, over-enthusiastic, jeepers-what-a-break-conducting-the-New-York-Philharmonic-at-last standard interpreter of the Tschaikowsky "Fourth." Then, when everybody, including the frustrated public, had completely given up hope, the stars or the vibra-tions or the Eustachian tubes did a switcheroo, and Toscanini announced he would conduct the last concert of the season. This was the famous Sunday-afternoon Beethoven concert at the Met-ropolitan Opera House which consisted of the "Eroica" and the "Ninth," and which they are still talking about.

It was just magnificent, that's all, and the or-chestra played way over their heads. In the slow movement John Fabriccio, one of the flute players, soaked his stiff bosom with tears, and everybody else in the orchestra was moved just the same way.

All the nice music-club ladies in the Schola Cantorum sang high G's pianissimo, like a whole chorus of Rethbergs and Jeritzas. . . .

The Maestro took only one bow, however, be-cause of the huge wreath which two ushers rushed down the aisle with, through the frantic and hysterically applauding audience. As he came out onto the stage for his first bow, there was this giant wreath bearing the legend: "From the Philharmonic Society." He looked at it with a dumfounded expression and rushed off the stage to his dressing room, where he locked himself in for two hours while the awe-struck, emotion-soaked, incoherent, shrieking audience, who had just heard what was undoubtedly the world's greatest performance of the "Ninth Symphony," screamed itself hoarse.

Through the keyhole Mrs. Toscanini pleaded with the Maestro to come out, but he didn't until the disappointed worshipers had all gone home. Only then did he unlock the dressing-room door and bundle himself back to the Astor, muttering, "Wreaths are for prima donnas and dead men!"

I guess there will never be another Toscanini, and everybody I know who ever played with him will say the same thing. Napoleon must have had somewhat the same genius for inspiring complete devotion among his troops. In the case of Toscanini, this devotion is mixed with an unreasoning fear also.

Like the troops on the transport ship in that famous cartoon who all marched overboard because their commanding officer was a stutterer and couldn't manage to say "Halt!" any of us in

Toscanini's orchestra would have unquestioningly done the same, though as much from reasons of being afraid of him as of loving him.

Not long ago Dr. Frank Black, the NBC musical director, performed a composition of mine. He very kindly mentioned this to Toscanini, who said he would like to see this piece.

Now of course I really wouldn't give very much to hear Arturo Toscanini conduct one of my compositions—only my Santa Anita stock which I bought at par, my five-year lease on my apartment, and possibly my right eye. So when I heard about it I took my score and sat half the night in the Los Angeles airport waiting for a seat on an eastbound plane, arrived haggard and unstrung in New York some twenty-three hours later, rushed to the Maestro's rehearsal at Radio City, paced up and down the halls till he finished with his rehearsal and his rubdown, and was ushered by my good friend, Dr. Black, into The Presence.

There were those eyes and they darted at me, around me, over me, and through me. That hoarse voice began:

"Ah yes, ah yes, ah yes—caro, caro, my dear, my dear—I remember, I remember—Willson, the flute, the flute, the American flute. You are now in California, no? With sunshine, the beautiful sunshine, and the oranges. You are well, no? You are happy? I am glad to see you. Ah yes, ah yes, ah yes—I remember, I remember."

Pause—long pause.

"Ah yes, ah yes—I remember—the American flute. Is always sun in California? I will come once to California, ah yes."

Pause.

"You wish to see me about something, no?"

I shook my head and bowed myself backward out of the dressing room with my score still under my arm. I hurried out to La Guardia Field, sat there half the night waiting for a seat on a west-bound plane, arrived in Los Angeles some twenty-three hours later, and I've never brought up the subject since.

Well, if you're an architect I can hear you stuttering and stammering in the presence of Frank Lloyd Wright. If you draw, I can see your flushed, self-conscious leer as you try to smile at Walt Disney. It's ridiculous, but being as I don't draw either houses or pictures, I could easily manage, "Good to see you, Frank," with customary Hollywood familiarity, and, "How are you, Walt?" with only the normal amount of quickening pulse reaction and pleasant anticipation caused by any important person. But my heart really stops beating at the thought of non-musicians giving the hand that has launched a thousand immortal down beats the old fraternity grasp accompanied by a cheery "Hiya doin', Art?"

And you know what I think? I think Toscanini would be a lot more comfortable and have more fun in the presence of some intelligent draftsman and imaginative cartoonists than he does with the cringing composers fumbling and fawning.

I've put these last observations down on the paper for my own benefit, to read and reread, so the next time—if there is a next time—that I get a chance to show one of my scores to Toscanini, I will have the good sense to let some nice architect take it back there for me.

16. ALONG ABOUT THIS TIME A VERY FINE dancer by the name of Angna Enters was planning to give a recital, and she asked me if I would like to hook on with the flute. Sort of a joint recital, as you might say—although, of course, what she had in her mind was that something had to go on while she was changing her costumes. But anyway I was glad of the opportunity because of the unwritten law that you aren't getting anyplace until you give some kind of recital, and all of the critics, including Olin Downes of the New York *Times*, were scheduled to be present.

Now you shouldn't hold grudges and everybody knows it, but still everybody goes right on holding grudges. The funny thing is that usually this person you have hated year after year has no idea you feel that way on account of nine times out of ten the thing he did to you was so slight and unintentional that it made no impression whatever in his mind. But all the time this "terrible affront" was running wild in your system like the devil grass back of the hen house, growing out of all proportion into a ridiculous snarl of a wiry, unreasonable, un-get-at-able, messy, matted mess.

You can be cured of this grudge nonsense if you ever get to realize that exactly as you are hating some pretty nice guy who doesn't know or even dream how you feel about him, somebody else is hating you for something you did so long ago you don't even remember it.

I was never so dumfounded as the day I got a letter with a Kankakee postmark that started off with a pencil diagram of South Superior Street in Mason City with all the houses labeled. There was the Collins house, then Old Man Birney, then the jog in the street, then the barn that was moved up to the sidewalk and made over into a bungalow, then Glanville's, then Malthouse's. Across the street was Brice's corner, then the Hughes girls, Norene and Regina, and then a house with an arrow pointing to it and this remark: "I've been hearing you on the radio, and if you are the Willson who lived in this house, I just want you to know you ruined the only chance I ever had of having a merry Christmas when I was little, and I've hated you for it ever since and always will."

I was full of all kinds of things, including righteous indignation, that this man didn't even sign his name and give me a chance to find out what in the hell was eating him. And then suddenly it hit me. Was *I* living in a glass house!

And so here I go dumping all my grudges into oblivion, including my special, gilt-edged, four-star, twenty-year-old hate against Olin Downes, music critic, and thank you, Kankakee! I will quote Mr. Downes's review of that recital for the last time, and I will then unbrand it from my brain and forgive and forget, so help me:

> *Miss Enters is perhaps the greatest mime of our day. As for the rest of the evening, its items were uniformly vapid.*

I hope my nobility and generosity in taking leave of this grudge are not entirely based upon the fact that flute playing isn't so important to me any more on account of I'm more interested in composing music.

Richard Wagner was allergic to wool socks. This is the only thing I have in common with Mr. Wagner so far—although I'm still trying to write something by way of music that might have a chance of lasting longer than I do.

Believing that nothing is impossible, I might accomplish this yet; and how did I arrive at this knowledge that *nothing* is impossible? I'll tell you.

Ever hear of Sammy Gardner? Well, you might say he was greater than Heifetz and Brahms put together. I mean Sammy was a skinny little kid like Heifetz was once, and they both played the fiddle. However, Heifetz was playing better fiddle than anybody in the world before he was old enough to blow his own nose. You couldn't have held back that flood of genius any more than you could have plugged up the cloudburst of melody that poured out of Brahms. Those two gents were gods all right, no question about it.

Sammy Gardner, on the other hand, was not from Olympus at all. He was not even from Olympus Junction. He was just a skinny little Human Being. That ain't by any means bad, though, is it, on account of there are godly heights to which any human being can rise if he gets desperate enough —and Sammy Gardner had one burning reason for living, and one only, and that was to compose and perform his own violin concerto with the New York Philharmonic Orchestra in Carnegie Hall. And that's the end of that story. You know without my telling you about the hours, days, weeks, months, years, skinnier legs, stronger glasses, living in shifts like a galley slave, pulling blood music out of a sea of fiddle guts with a horsehair oar, pounding dull, dull, dust-dry rules, between shifts, into that small round button of a non-smiling dogged little desperate little schoolboy head already bursting with scales, chords, counterpoint, harmony, theory.

Did he make it? Are you kidding? I was playing the flute with the New York Philharmonic the night that Samuel Gardner, Human Being, walked out onto the stage of Carnegie Hall to play his own violin concerto. Nobody helped him to that triumph but himself. The only strings to that show were on his fiddle. You might say he was greater than Heifetz and Brahms put together.

17. IT WAS NOW 1928 AND I HAD KNOWN
for several years a remarkable man named Adolph
Linden, who was building a national radio chain.
In the twenties there was only one complete
coast-to-coast network, and it was highly desirable
to broadcast not only east to west, but also west
to east, and this network-reversing was a big tech-
nical chore and expensive, too, in those days, so
Mr. Linden thought of having *his* coast-to-coast
station hooked together in a figure-eight pattern, so that the broadcast would constantly be
flowing in both directions at once and no network
reversals would ever be necessary.

He invited me to Seattle one week end to see if
I would fit into the musical plans of this proposed
broadcasting, and I was pretty excited about the
whole thing and met a bunch of nice people, including a young drummer—a sort of northwest
Phil Harris—who was organizing the dance-band
programs for Mr. Linden's Seattle station, KJR.
This drummer had a fine café orchestra on the

side, and one day to brighten things up a little, also as a publicity stunt, he thought he would run for mayor. Down at the City Hall they told him that the ticket was full, but there was also a state election coming up and would he like to run for something on that? The Democratic ticket was open, as usual, since nobody had bothered to run against the Republicans up there in Washington since the Civil War.

So our young drummer friend said, "Whadaya got?" and the clerk at the City Hall said, "How'd you like to run for lieutenant-governor?" and the drummer said, "Jake with me—write 'er down."

And he started his campaign, complete with open barouche, top hat, baby kissing, and two highly original planks in his platform which were: "A Flowerpot on Every Hydrant," and "A Pretty Girl on Every Streetcar."

And wouldn't you know that that was the year of the Democratic landslide, and before you could say "New Deal," Vic Meyers, the café drummer, had become lieutenant-governor. Victor A. Meyers of the state of Washington, and if you thought that could only happen in Hollywood you're wrong.

And listen to this: the Honorable Victor Meyers did not turn out to be the second bass clarinet player of the Washington State Senate by any means. He boned up on procedures and took hold of his job and has been re-elected clear up to this very day and is as popular as any lieutenant-governor any state ever had.

Sometimes Mr. Linden must have felt like Pygmalion—and incidentally, like Houdini—for he changed my flute into a baton when he decided to give summer symphonies in Seattle, like the Bowl concerts in Hollywood, and engaged me as his musical director.

Well, this seemed a good time to get my picture taken, so what with the new conducting job and all, I decided to go first-class, and I hunted up practically the most famous photographer in New York City at the time, whose studio was on Park Avenue—man named Townsend.

It turned out to be the dangedest, most gorgeous bunch of potted palms, soft lights, and trick mirrors you've ever seen in your whole born days. I leaned against a fountain and waited for somebody to come in.

A very continentalish sort of a pince-nez type gentleman came in presently and started to visit. After about fifteen minutes of this I said, "Excuse me, but I have to go to rehearsal. Are you about ready to start taking my picture?"

"My dear boy, I've taken fourteen already and I think we should get one or two out of that, don't you?"

I apologized and said, "This is all new stuff to me—in fact, I haven't had my picture taken since Uncle Ed's funeral in Charles City."

The gentleman fell into the nearest chair. "Charles City! Why, I used to work right across the street from the Hildreth Hotel. Prettiest little river in the whole state running across Main Street. Why, I only left there maybe fifteen years ago! They tell me the John Deere Company's got a brand-new building down by the depot!"

Well, whadayaknow, that's Iowa for you.

To get back from the photograph to the occasion for the photograph, I had positively left the Philharmonic and the flute-playing business in order to conduct for Mr. Adolph Linden, who had planned this outdoor concert season particularly to advertise his new network.

We made elaborate and expensive preparations, including a hundred thousand dollars' worth of musicians imported from New York. The weather man double-crossed us, however, and we laid a very large egg in the shadow of Mount Rainier, to one cold and gloomy audience after another, and besides, Mr. Linden had very high and idealistic principles which sometimes don't help the cash register, and before he knew it, the pressure was on him and what might well have been the second coast-to-coast network folded up and I was back in New York again trying to pick up the pieces—

which included the hundred thousand dollars' worth of musicians' contracts with my name signed to them.

The first Sunday I was back I was offered a job playing as a "sospitute" in the band in Central Park. It only paid ten bucks, but I thought coming down to earth after my Seattle fling would be good for the soul, as you might say, so I grabbed it, and fortunately my old Sousa uniform still fit after a fashion. Unfortunately, however, I had told a couple of friends about the concert I was "doing" in the park, and with characteristic human frailty I'm afraid I indicated that I was conducting the band instead of playing in it, being careful, of course, to avoid mentioning *what* park. But they found out and all filed in just in time for the first encore, which was "The Stars and Stripes Forever"—and there I stood with my piccolo.

Within the next few days, however, every one of the boys I had signed for the Seattle venture had torn up their contracts and wished me luck, leaving me in the great-while-it-lasted-better-luck-next-time department, which gave me spunk enough to put away the flute and piccolo and scram to California and start my second career from scratch. Thank you very much, all you guys.

Isn't that the way it goes? Just when I'm getting used to New York—in fact, beginning to consider myself a New Yorker who could never live anyplace *but*—I find myself headin' West like my Watertown Grampa before me, only by train instead of by ox team, and to Cali-for-ni-ay instead of to Ioway (may Senator Hickenlooper forgive me), and just when I've learned to drop a couple *r*'s like a natural-born New Yorker without feeling self-conscious.

New Yorkers also say "bunk" instead of "bump," like "I bunked into an old friend." And there's no such thing as brick cheese in New York, or a New York cut steak, for that matter. And New Yorkers say, "Two and a half dollars" instead of "Two dollars and a half." Also "singles" for dollar bills, "store cheese" for "rat cheese," and anything you buy in bulk is "loose," like loose milk and loose crackers. Nobody in New York eats crackers and milk, though, like everybody did in Iowa, just before going to bed. Iowans also like ginger snaps and a miserable oblongish brown cooky called "Helen" or "Mary Ann" which my brother Cedric and I ate only as an absolute last resort. We even preferred bitter cooking chocolate, which wasn't bad with a big spoonful of sugar.

Nothing was as bitter, though, as when you'd pick a long dandelion, split the end, and run the stem up against your tongue to make "dandy-line curls." Can't you taste it, hmmm? Tastes are just as nostalgic as sounds, I guess.

How about the times when you made your face up like a circus clown or an Apache on the warpath? You'd use your long shiny black box of water colors (tell the truth now—when there wasn't any water handy didn't you sometimes "pit" in it?), and when you were painting your face, maybe you'd accidentally get the brush too close to your mouth, remember? Can't you taste it? And can't you taste the masks you used to wear on Halloween? (New York kids wear them on Thanksgiving, too, and go around ringing doorbells, saying, "Something for Thanksgiving?")

And that great big penny stick of licorice after you'd used it all day as a whip . . .

And the flashlight batteries we used to taste with our tongue . . .

And the leather mittens! (Don't know what they were doing in my mouth, come to think of it, but I can sure taste 'em right now) . . .

And the soap from your soap-bubble pipe when you inhaled by mistake. Papa used to put ammonia in the water to make colored bubbles, and speaking of colored bubbles, open your eyes, kids —here we are in California.

18. WHILE I WAS WAITING FOR A TAXICAB
in the Pasadena railroad station (Hollywood
doesn't have a railroad station—doesn't even have
a railroad) I met a small girl who said she'd never
be able to leave home on account of she lived in
the middle of an orange grove, and if she ever
moved away she'd be homesick for the sound of
the orange blossoms falling in the night. I thought
that was a pretty poetic remark.

A large hunk of the Hollywood glamour group,
by the way, goes through Pasadena for another
reason than the railroad station—in order to get
to the race track at Santa Anita. But somehow
Pasadenians are just simply invulnerable to that
fancy Hollywood star dust, which doesn't seem to
brush off onto them at all. They are just as natural
and unaffected as a crock of beans at a church
social.

A crock of beans at a church social. A thought
like that can sure juicy-up your memory, can't it?

Like Von Weber, the great composer, who couldn't write for sour apples until he went over to the piano and hit D and F sharp. Then he was a ball of fire. Well, I want to tell you that crock of beans has D-and-F-sharped me right back to Mason City again, and California will have to wait, because I'm on my way down-cellar to sprout the potatoes, or to get a jar of ground cherries, or to bust up some ice in the gunny sack with the ax to make ice cream. Just smell that stone-cool cellar smell.

It smelled even cooler on rainy Saturday afternoons when the wash had to be hung out in the "laundry." Later on, after helping with the wringer and all, provided we were careful with the lace doilies, Mama'd let us get out the buffalo robe and throw it down on the sitting-room floor. I never knew then that those lace things were called "doilies," though. In fact, somehow or other I left Mason City believing that doily was kind of a dirty word. In fact, I guess the only reason I brought it up now was because I get sort of a vicarious thrill using it so freely—doily doily doily.

Anyway, we loved to scramble around on the buffalo robe and invent things with our Meccano set and rubber bands and marbles and the wooden fire engine with the big heavy momentum wheel in its bottom. We didn't have any jigsaw puzzles then, but there was a puzzle with big honest pieces that made a picture of a river steamboat when we put it together. Never got tired of doing it over and over. The blue sky was the hardest part, and the rail around the boat and the paddle wheel were the easiest.

Like doily, "powerhouse" always had a self-conscious significance, but there was a reason for that on account of the boys' toilet was in the powerhouse at school. "Miss Wallacer, can I go to the powerhouse?" So even at home, going to the bathroom was, "Have to go to the powerhouse."

I wonder if kids still get coupons at the bookstore for secondhand books. What a racket we used to put over on Papa every single summer. We'd take all the schoolbooks we could find and get coupons for them and trade these coupons for hard rubber balls or slingshot rubbers or "glassies" or "steelies" or "pig turds." (I can see Miss Remley now, patiently standing behind the marbles counter saying, "Now let's see, you wanted—uh—ten of the peewees, that one large glassie, six snot-agates, and three of the pig turds." I'm only telling you what everybody called the different kinds of marbles and I'm not mistaken. I remember distinctly.) We'd get all that stuff instead of the books for next term. Then in the fall Papa would have to cough up for books all over again. Why don't parents drown their kids?

Roger Glanville was a little older than the other

kids on our block, but never mind age—he just had a natural talent for organizing. When I think of Rog, even now, I think of him sprawling on a rich diamond-and-ruby-studded throne, being transported from place to place by generous and willing sycophants. Not that Rog lorded it over us at all—he was smarter than we were and he used us to his own comfort and advantage and we knew it and loved it.

It was Rog who flattered and encouraged Heckie Mackett into building a long sort of shuffleboard table with his uncle's lumber and his father's tools. At the end of this table there were six or seven round depressions. These holes were numbered, and prizes with corresponding numbers were set up in a showcase on Roger's coaster wagon. You rolled the rubber balls—three rolls for a dime—down the table toward the holes. If, by some miracle, a ball stayed in one of those holes, you got the prize the number called for.

No, Roger didn't furnish the prizes—of course not. Every kid in the neighborhood brought things from home and freely and happily lavished them on Rog the Brain, to be used for the prizes. These things were liable to be anything from a piece of your mother's Haviland china to a couple of links pried out of Grampa's silver log-chain, and if Rog was pleased that was all the pay we wanted.

Of course we also supplied him with the rubber

balls which we got from Miss Remley with coupons. All Rog did was to sit on his front porch and ballyhoo the game. He was a natural-born barker, and considering the setup, it mattered not to Rog whether the suckers won a prize or didn't —his take was exactly the same—one hundred per cent. Nobody would think of asking this mental giant to split the profits.

His self-operating strokes of genius included "allowing" us to peddle bills for his father's dry-goods store in return for a ride to the outskirts of town in the store's four-cylinder Hupmobile truck, which could be converted into a runabout at the end of the day. He collected fifty cents a head on us while we were walking back peddling the bills and extolling Roger's generosity for giving us such a nice long ride.

Then there was our "Wild West Fireworks Display." The biggest event in any kid's life, of course, was the Paine's Fireworks on the last night of the county fair in September. We were always a little bored in the grandstand during the daytime on account of the sulky races, but for some reason Papa always wanted us to see them. Wholesome, I guess. There was, of course, the relief of the band music and the acrobats between heats. And then the final glorious fireworks climax of "The Last Days of Pompeii" (everybody back home said Pom-pee-eye), or "The San Francisco

Earthquake," or just spectacular things like elephants and Niagara Falls.

Well, one spring Rog found out that Heckie Mackett's uncle was in the wholesale fireworks business and also had some old Paine's Fireworks posters, and this knowledge started a chain of events that ended with the entire hillside below Igou's pasture being sold out at twenty-five cents a ticket to adults yet, who came from all over town to see my brother Cedric, my cousin Phil, Art Swanson, Shink Burns, and Jody Farrell, in water-color war paint, tear down the hill to the creek in an old gocart with a little cheesecloth tacked on to represent a prairie schooner. Heckie's uncle didn't come through, after all, with anything but the posters, and our fireworks display turned out to be two packages of firecrackers that didn't go off and three Roman candles that fortunately set fire to the old oak tree, and by the time the audience helped to put it out, the lack of actual entertainment was more or less forgotten. Roger's profit was again a hundred per cent. We even got the firecrackers and Roman candles for him from the bookstore with coupons.

In the wintertime there were snow-shoveling expeditions where we all labored after school for Ol' Massa Rog. He got the jobs for us and collected the money and paid us off in ten-cent hatchets from Woolworth's—that is, everybody except me. My brother Cedric had the seniority rights on our snow shovel, so all I could do was bring up the rear with the broom and sweep up, to make the job look neat. So I only got a hammer instead of a hatchet.

But the master stroke of Roger's entire career was when he organized the "South Superior Street Boy Scouts of America."

Mason City had heard a lot about Dan Beard and the Boy Scout movement, but there was as yet no accredited camp established with an authorized scout leader and all. Musing on this on his front porch one day, Rog sent a runner (me) to round up his faithful subjects, who girded on their hatchets and came flying.

The first step was for us all to go up into the north side and display our hatchets, mumbling at the same time something about our Boy Scout camp. The next move was for us all to descend on Mr. Muse, the editor of the *Globe-Gazette*, who was a pushover for kids, and ask him to run an announcement in the paper that anyone wishing to be a Boy Scout should come to Glanville's barn on South Superior Street at ten o'clock Saturday morning.

By now every kid in town was in a furor and Rog hadn't moved off his front porch. He had his coup timed perfectly and his "avenue of retreat" all figured out too. What a marshal he would have made for Napoleon.

The events transpired thusly. Saturday morning every kid from six to sixteen was fighting to get into Glanville's barn. Rog collected a quarter membership fee, painted a cross on each kid's forehead with red water colors, and stuck a hatchet in each kid's pants and made him an S.S.S.B.S.A. By an unlucky coincidence, the following Monday an official Boy Scout movement was launched from the Lincoln School, and the following Saturday, South Superior Street was full of screaming kids with hatchets, yelling to get their quarters back. My cousin Phil and I hid in Grampa's corncrib till dark. My brother Cedric holed up in our secret cigarette factory under the Willow Creek Bridge. Roger, of course, was on his way to visit his aunt for the usual two-week trip his folks always took every summer to Galena, Illinois.

He came back with a fascinating plan to organize the South Superior Street Pushmobile Society, which he had worked out in complete detail, including official membership cards stamped S.S.S.P.S. which he had allowed his cousin in Galena to print for him. These cards only cost you a nominal entrance fee of twenty-five cents and permitted you to wear your cap backward at all times.

19. ABE MEYER, MY GOOD FRIEND AND THE fellow who helped to get me my first publisher, was now musical director of Tiffany-Stahl, a Hollywood picture company. I deposited my transfer card in the local musicians' union and went to see Abe. He said I could help him at the studio in various odd things and do some picture scoring and conducting later on.

In those days (early 1929) Hollywood was a glorified fish fry, and the important thing was to look busy, so at Abe's suggestion I took up cigar smoking and spent my mornings walking around the Tiffany-Stahl lot, knitting my brows and smoking cigars.

I scored some of the music for the talking version of *Peacock Alley* with Mae Murray, and a horrible thing called *The Lost Zeppelin* with Conway Tearle. Didn't know much about picture scoring—in fact, didn't know *anything* about picture scoring—but my cigar gave out the proper smoke screen.

I went up to San Francisco to see a football game and ran into a heck of a talented girl I had met in Seattle by the name of Merle Matthews. She was writing programs for the Don Lee radio station, KFRC, at that time, and introduced me to Harrison Holloway and Fred Pabst, the managers. We hit it off just fine and they hired me as musical director of the station.

One of our big radio shows was called *Captain Dobbsie's Ship of Joy*. Dobbsie was a wonderful fellow full of inspiration and sweetness—and full of a slight tendency to forget where he parked his car—or parked his hat—or parked Mrs. Dobbsie. On one of his programs he had as his guest an eminent ethnologist who had just returned from the South Sea Islands, and with him he brought a lala, not to be confused with a lulu. This lala was made from the trunk of a tree and was about sixty-five feet long. When the natives hit it, it gave out a deep throbbing sound that carried for ninety or a hundred miles. It was used as a sort of telegraph, and when the natives in the next village picked up the beat, they'd relay the messages on *their* lalas to other villages, and pretty soon it got noised all through the South Seas that Montgomery Ward was selling men's underwear at seventy-nine cents, or whatever they wanted to noise all through the South Seas.

Well, came time for the broadcast. Before hitting the lala, Dobbsie asked the listeners to go down in their cellars or up in the attic or out in the garage—he wanted to prove that the sound of the lala was so penetrating that no matter how far away they went from their radio sets they'd hear it anyway.

"While you're getting there," Dobbsie said, "the orchestra will play a tune," which we did, whereupon Dobbsie went into a talk about the ancient Peruvian stone carvers—and completely forgot everything else. That was fifteen years ago, and so far as I know those poor people are still in their cellars and attics, waiting for the sound of the lala. . . .

Dobbsie had a lot of guest stars, including Nina Koshetz, who sang "Estrellita" with the *Ship of Joy* orchestra, not, however, before indulging herself in a lifelong ceremonial which consisted of breaking—literally *breaking*—the neck of a bottle of champagne over the microphone and drinking a toast to "Orpheus," Dobbsie, the orchestra, and the astonished engineer, who was not exactly prepared for a real "glass-crash" sound effect within such startling proximity to his beloved equipment.

On that same program I learned that Josef Lhévinne could really set your cork a-bobbin' with Chopin's "F-Minor Concerto"—also, that the bigger the artist, the easier he is to work with—and if they're like Mr. Lhévinne they are courteous and mild and kindly and gentle. Mr. Lhévinne's gentleness turned into uncompromising steel, however, the moment the performance began and the chips were down. He sat at that piano like a granite mountain till the last note was played, and then he instantly relaxed into the modest, almost apologetic personality that was so characteristic of this great man.

I also learned that a blond young Philadelphian named Nelson Eddy was getting good and tired of hanging around M.G.M. doing bit parts and was happy to get away to San Francisco and get a chance to sing again. He was barely in his twenties, but he killed all the people with the most tastefully complete singing of the "Toreador Song" you'll ever want to hear. He was a bit on the callow side in those days, as it comes to me now. Having met Dr. Alfred Hertz of the San Francisco Symphony and Dr. Gaetano Merola of the San Francisco Opera during his stay, he concluded that "Doctor" was synonymous with "Maestro" or "Conductor," and he naïvely proceeded to call me Doctor during the rest of his visit, which, I may say, aroused my great embarrassment—not to mention the orchestra's sadistic sense of humor.

San Francisco was the key radio town of the Coast in those days and had lots of potential stuff simmering. Al Pearce had a daytime show at KFRC. Over at the St. Francis Hotel a curly-haired drummer by the name of Phil Harris of the Loughner-Harris orchestra was causing talk. He came to my office one day and said approximately: "Mare" (that's what my name sounds like when they shorten it), "I gotta get on this long-hair-style band leading. Three-four and four-four and all that difficult stuff—I don't wanna conduct with my feet all my life. Now I've got a little time on my hands this morning, a half-hour anyway. Would you do your old pal a favor? Hand me one of your batons and teach me to conduct right now."

Phil has been natural like that all his life. Shows you how being yourself pays off.

The "lesson" only lasted fifteen minutes, by the way. Phil got restless.

San Francisco certainly did all right by the dance-band profession. Not only Phil, but Art Hickman, Paul Whiteman, Ted Fio Rito, Tom Coakley, Carl Ravazza, Jim Walsh, Horace Heidt, Anson Weeks, and Tom Gerun either got their start or became famous there. Tom settled down to the restaurant business, going into a big project with Frank Martinelli called the Bal Tabarin. Shortly after they opened Tom decided he'd rather stand out in the lobby and smile than stand on the bandstand and smile and have to monkey around with the sixteenth notes besides, so he brought in a green young band from some college town back East. The day they opened Tom asked me to stop by in the afternoon to listen to the orchestra balance, as they were planning to broadcast this new band over NBC that night. I climbed up to a dinky little improvised beaverboard control room over the kitchen and listened for a while, and everything sounded fine except the guitar, which I couldn't hear at all, so I went down to the stage and condescendingly explained to the young leader in considerable detail that it was necessary to seat your rhythm section near the microphone, particularly the guitar on account of its light quality of tone. After all, it was important that those guitar afterbeats be distinct, etc., etc.

The young man listened politely, and when I got all through he said, "Please, suh, thank you, suh, but Ah don't use any guitar in dis heah band." And he excused himself and continued with the rehearsal like this: "Come on, chillun. Yet's go!" Yeah—Kay Kyser.

Over at NBC down on Sutter Street they had a fine radio stock company, including an ambitious write named Carlton Morse, who wrote practically everybody at the station into a serial called *One Man's Family*, which later moved to Hollywood with the whole original cast. Bill Goodwin was one of the staff announcers at KFRC and up on the Hill at the Mark, a Latin fiddler named Xavier

Cugat was playing intermission solos for Anson Weeks's orchestra.

Carmen Castillo, a lovely singer, was also at the Mark and we built a Spanish program around her at KFRC. She wanted to bring her niece to play castanets, excepting the niece was too young to join the union, so I invited the little girl to the broadcast and let her sit in the front row (near a microphone) and told her if she happened to bring her castanets and was carried away by the music and just couldn't resist playing along, I didn't see how anyone could stop her, and besides, Al Greenbaum down at Local 6 was a real nice reasonable fellow. She did and it was very pretty and so was she. You saw her in *Lost Horizon*, and her name is Margo.

Over in Oakland a young high school boy was fascinated with the radio goings on and was dreaming about some kind of program where you could get the people in the audience to participate and maybe give away prizes. He turned out to be Ralph "Truth or Consequences" Edwards.

But the big show in those days was *The Blue Monday Jamboree*, a two-hour clambake every Monday night from eight to ten, and you could shoot off a gun in any street in California on that night and never hit anybody on account of they were all home listening to *The Blue Monday Jamboree*. I can't think of anything that's ever been done on the radio that we didn't do first on that program.

Amos 'n' Andy? We had Lem and Lafe. (In fact, we had Amos 'n' Andy as guests once, only they were then called Sam 'n' Henry.)

Lum and Abner? We had Ed and Zeb.

Mortimer Snerd? We had Elmer Blurt.

Mel Blanc's characters? We had Pedro, the Mexican janitor, Frank Watanabe, and Simpy Fitts.

Stoopnagle and Budd? We had Yahbut and Cheerily.

Gene Autry? We had Haywire Mack.

We had our own comedy stock company. We played the first original musical comedies ever written for the air. We did murder mysteries and burlesque whodunits.

Mr. Bunce, the janitor of the building, was also our sound-effects man. He invented his own paraphernalia, and so far as I know was the first one to figure out that a bunch of little wooden blocks hung from a square frame on a string netting would sound like a company of marching men.

Ferde Grofé wrote a piece for piano called "Metropolis" which Dave Tamkin orchestrated for our *Jamboree* orchestra, and I wanted to use realistic street noises such as a rivet gun.

"The only thing that'll sound like a rivet gun," Mr. Bunce said, "is a rivet gun."

He got one and hooked it up to a tankful of compressed air. We didn't have time to rehearse it on account of we only used to have an hour rehearsal for a two-hour broadcast in those days, so I told Mr. Bunce to start the riveter when I raised my hand, and stop when I dropped it.

"Metropolis" was the first piece on the program and we were going fine until the climax, when the rivet gun was supposed to come in. I raised my hand and Mr. Bunce tried to start the gun, but something went haywire and nothing happened till we had finished the entire piece and then, just as I gave the last down beat, in came the riveter with a terrific roar which didn't get shut off until a hour-hour after the broadcast was over. And I guess on that particular night The Blue Monday Jamboree was fairly confusing for the listeners-in, not to say monotonous.

We used to dedicate each Monday to a certain profession or industry. Came railroad trainmen night on the Jamboree. Mr. Holloway, who not only managed the station but emceed its ace programs, thought it would be a fine idea to interview a locomotive engineer and ask him what the various train whistles meant. And somebody else thought it would be an even finer idea if we put a locomotive whistle right in the studio and let him demonstrate on it.

We got in touch with a crack engineer on the

Southern Pacific and he took the steam whistle right off his engine and had it hauled to the studio, all four hundred and seventy-five pounds of it, and we connected it to Mr. Bunce's compressed-air tank and hooked the trigger up to a clothesline we strung right over the microphone.

Now, as I said, we didn't bother much with rehearsals in those days. We merely put the show on the air and hoped for the best. So Monday night the audience came in and the *Jamboree* got started, and pretty soon it was time for the engineer and his whistle.

Mr. Holloway, as the emcee, asked him what was his favorite whistle and he said, "Three longs and a short—that lets my wife know she can start fixing breakfast—I'm only fifty miles up the line."

Now wouldn't you have thought that somebody would have realized that you shouldn't take a whistle you can hear for fifty miles and blow it in a radio studio? But nobody did.

"Well," Mr. Holloway said, "how does it go?" And the engineer reached up and yanked the clothesline.

The whistle blew, all the windows in the studio fell in, the roof collapsed, the station went off the air for two weeks, and twenty people sued us for broken eardrums. Ever since that time whenever I hear *Casey Jones* I shudder a little.

Well, Don Lee began to see the Hollywood

handwriting on the wall and moved his radio headquarters to KHJ in Los Angeles, but I stayed in San Francisco and moved down the street to become musical director of the NBC stations, KGO and KPO.

I had visited Abe Meyer in Hollywood now and again and he had criticized me for not playing enough of the current popular tunes, so just to quiet him down and also to start off my new job with a new program idea, I took the ten most-played songs of the week out of *Variety's* list and made them into a show called *The Big Ten.*

A bright lad named Don Forker, who was working for the Lord and Thomas Advertising Agency at the time, came to California on his vacation and heard the show, which was pretty popular with the Cal and Stanford kids by now. He went back to New York and sold the show to George Washington Hill for Lucky Strike, and they put it on NBC as the *Lucky Strike Hit Parade,* and it has been on the air ever since.

No, I did not get a cool million for it, nor a hundred thousand, nor a few G's maybe, nor a C-note, a sawbuck, a fin, a carton of Luckies, or even a puff. You see, Mr. Hill said the agency sold him the show, so I should take it up with the agency, and the agency said they had the network's blessing, go take it up with NBC. NBC said I was their employee and my ideas were theirs to give away if they so desired, but they were sorry, at least, and they have certainly gone out of their way to be extra nice to me ever since, and I'm sure it was all for the best, and I'm not too crazy about the program anyway, and besides, I'll get another idea someday.

Meanwhile I was busy with another show called *The Carefree Carnival*, which featured Tim and Irene, Susie at the switchboard, Charlie Marshall, Vera Vague, the "little king of song" Tommy Harris, Pinky Lee, and Jerry Lester. We also had a non-stop musical called *America Sings*, *Chiffon Jazz*, *Waltz Time*, and a weekly half-hour for the Bank of America called *House of Melody*, in which I split the billing with a local boy named John Nesbitt, who did the commentating. He was good.

The NBC studios were on the twenty-second floor, and it was pretty inspiring to look out of the windows and watch the beginning of the world's greatest bridge, and it finally gnawed at me to the extent that I started to write a symphony (appropriately titled Symphony Number One—also known as "The San Francisco Symphony")— measure for cable, note for rivet—and what surprised me even more, I finished it neck and neck with the ribbon-cutting ceremony. The bridge, however, made more money.

20. SAN FRANCISCO HAS MORE PERSON-
ality than any other city I've ever been in: big,
good, kind, friendly, the Golden Gate, the food,
the people, their appreciation of music and
sculpture and honest art, hills, the Family Club,
the Bohemian Club, Dr. Margaret Chung—ask
any flier about Margaret Chung—Julius's Castle,
Golden Gate Park, the Opera House, the fine
musicians, the symphony, and Pierre Monteux.

I sure do admire Monsieur Monteux. He only
knows me as a composer, although I played the
flute under him when he guest-conducted in New
York in my Philharmonic days. He is one of the
world's great conductors and has made the San
Francisco Symphony one of the great orchestras
of our time. His music comes first, and that's
honest with him—not a pose. Ask the photog-
raphers and interviewers who try to see him on a
rehearsal day. On other days he's full of charm
and graciousness and stories.

He was conducting in Paris a certain year when the symphony players were pretty independent, as they had a lot of outside work like the Folies-Bergère and the hotels that were more lucrative than the long-haired jobs—so every rehearsal, Monsieur Monteux would see different faces among the players, until by the last rehearsal everyone in the orchestra had sent a substitute but the timpani player, whom Monsieur Monteux addressed as follows:

"You, sir, the timpanist, you have attended the rehearsals faithfully."

"Thank you, sir."

"Every one of them."

"Thank you, sir."

"In fact, you are the only member of this orchestra who has personally attended every rehearsal, and I want to express to you my special thanks and extreme appreciation."

"Thank you, sir. Uh—Monsieur Monteux——"

"Yes?"

"My only regret is that I will be unable to play at the concert tonight."

Well, I was very happy in San Francisco and proud, too, on account of a "Meredith Willson Day" that the mayor hung on me after my first symphony was played.

Are you self-conscious when the photographer

asks you for one of those handshaking poses and you have to look somebody in the eye for five or ten minutes before the picture is snapped? Well, believe me, I am. Herb Caen—now why in the world should anybody spell Cane like that?— Herb Caen, a remarkable San Francisco newspaperman, told me one time that it's very easy to "cheat" in such a shot by looking slightly higher, at the person's forehead. Then the picture looks like you are looking right at them and nobody's embarrassed. So that day at the City Hall I thought I'd try it. The only trouble was that the mayor was bald as a grapefruit, and when the picture came out it didn't look eye-to-eye at all. It looked like I was doing just what I was doing: inspecting His Honor's hairless dome with considerable astonishment. And if I'm ever invited to the City Hall again I'll be very surprised and no thanks to you, Herb Caen.

Anyway, I was sorry to see radio's headquarters unmistakably pushing southward to Los Angeles. But one day a young man by the name of George Gruskin, who didn't look a day older than twenty-three but who was actually only twenty-two, came to San Francisco representing the William Morris office. He wanted to know if I had an agent, and I said no, and by the time his plane left for Los Angeles that night I had one and he was it, and before the year was out I was in Hollywood on the

Maxwell House radio program, partly because of this George Gruskin, partly because of a tall thin Mormon.

Every Mormon I ever knew was a wonderful person, and that goes for the King Sisters.

This tall thin Mormon named Don Cope was a mighty fine producer at NBC in San Francisco, but he went to New York to work for Benton and Bowles, which is an advertising agency that put on the Maxwell House radio program, and Don Cope became the producer of it, and that's how he and I met again in Hollywood. And I've been with the Morris office, including George Gruskin, Bill Murray, and Abe Lastfogel, ever since, with a handshake for a contract. That's the best kind—there aren't any loopholes in a handshake.

But I always hate leaving San Francisco even on paper. Up there they say "Sa-uh-cisco." Everybody pronounces the name of his home town with a special little twist, or have you noticed? A native son down in Los Angeles says "Losannelus." Back home we hated you if you called Mason City "Mason"—like San Franciscans won't even answer you if you say "Frisco," and they really do simultaneously wear straw hats and overcoats and carry pocketfuls of half dollars.

But it's a different world up there. Is it the people, or the architecture, or the seven hills, or the bay, or Joe DiMaggio, or what? There must have been gloomy days when I lived there, but I don't remember them. You could set your watch by the four o'clock fog rolling in, which didn't make things gloomy, only cozy, or strong, or moving, or wild, or beautiful, or friendly.

Saturday afternoons happen every place, I guess, but not like those San Francisco ones when you're late going to lunch and you think everybody's left the office for the week end, and then you hear a paper rattle next door and it's Lew just about to call it a day. And you start chewing the rag and Mac comes in from the sales department and Harry says, "I wonder if that Christmas scotch is still in this bottom drawer." And somebody goes down the hall for Dixie cups and that's all, brother.

At a quarter to nine that night you're telling the chef at the Fly-Trap that he "makes the best li'l ol' spaghetti in the entire wessern hemi—hemi —in the entire world."

We used to have some two-fisted celebrators at the Family Club—Joe and Al Ghirardelli, Tim Pfleuger, Fred Sherman—but cocktail hour or midnight, if anyone sat down at the piano or got up to sing you could hear a pin drop. I never ran into this tradition in any other club.

Maybe they just like music up there in San Francisco. Maybe it's appreciation, or maybe only being sentimental. Maybe it's the difference between "Emperor" Norton and "Prince" Mike Romanoff. Maybe it's the history and the tradition of that happy peninsula, and then again maybe it's just the climate. Maybe it's the sound of the names of the streets: Sutter, Fremont, the Embarcadero, Dolores—or maybe it's just the wind.

Maybe it's all the extremes standing like giant parentheses from ocean to bay and embracing all the flashings of that "spiritual personality that is San Francisco." Maybe it *is* those extremes, after all, like the overcoats and straw hats, palm trees and steam heat, Gianninis and longshoremen, Stanford and Cal, ferryboats and the Golden Gate Bridge, cable cars and Treasure Island helicopters, the Palace Hotel and the Barbary Coast, the Queen Anne fronts and the Mary Jane backs.

Or maybe it's just the fog.

21. THE PROGRAM I WENT TO HOLLY-
wood to do was called *The Maxwell House Show
Boat from Hollywood*, which was rather odd be-
cause they had spent the preceding five years try-
ing to convince the radio audience that the
Maxwell House Show Boat actually plied the
Mississippi River from Natchez to Mobile, from
Memphis to St. Joe, wherever the four winds blow.

Anyway, the glittering, glamorous New York
advertising agency known as Benton and Bowles,
who had dreamed up *Captain Henry's Show Boat*
in the first place and who are the Brains behind
some of the biggest programs ever to bring thirty
thousand dollars' worth of talent every week into
your living room free for the tuning, started moving the pawns around on the radio chessboard,
which means they had changed their minds about
this *Hollywood Show Boat* and were now looking
for a new program for Maxwell House.

Mr. Benton and Mr. Bowles had met in college

days, incidentally, and decided to go into partnership and make a million dollars each by the time they were thirty-five and retire. Isn't that the silliest thing you ever heard of? What actually happened was that when they got to be thirty-five they had made a million dollars each and retired. Mr. Benton is William Chicago U Benton, and Mr. Bowles is Chester OPA Bowles.

So Benton and Bowles was being run by a remarkable man named Atherton W. Hobler, who came to Hollywood to see about replacing *Show Boat*, and he talked M.G.M. into a marriage with Maxwell House coffee, and the result was the radio program called *Good News*, and I went along with the deal.

It was too bad to see the old *Show Boat* fold. It had certainly been a milestone in radio entertainment and had discovered Nadine Connor, Lanny Ross, Thomas L. Thomas, Annette Henshaw, and lots of others. And the *Hollywood Show Boat*, even though it didn't last long, had been no slouch either, with Charlie Winninger, Hattie McDaniel, Jack Haley, Virginia Verrill, and Warren Hull.

I'll never forget the opening night of that *Hollywood Show Boat*. We broadcast from Stage Three on the Warner Brothers lot, as practically no radio studios had been built in Hollywood as yet. If you remember how the old *Show Boat* used to open, the first thing was a paddle-wheel sound effect with a calliope and then the chorus and the orchestra: "Here comes the show boat, here comes the show boat, puff puff Puff Puff PUFF *PUFF PUFFIN'* ALONG!"

That opening night, the studio clock was a minute and a half slow, so we were actually on the air a minute and a half before anybody realized it except the engineer, who frantically signaled from the booth, but nobody saw him except the sound-effects man. So the long-awaited, glamorous *Hollywood Show Boat* opened up with a minute-and-a-half cadenza for paddle wheel accompanied by a few confusing remarks: "Good luck, Charlie old boy," "Give 'em hell, Hattie," "Well, this is it, kid, all the best." It sure was funny, or at least it is now to look back on.

But that was nothing to the first *Good News* broadcast as produced by a very remarkable man named Bill Bacher. M.G.M. had taken over what is now the Paramount Theatre across the street from the Hollywood Hotel and rebuilt the stage into a replica of the Old Maxwell House in Nashville, complete with a crystal chandelier and forty or fifty thousand dollars' worth of gates and prop butlers serving Maxwell House coffee.

We had lots of glamour and had rehearsed for many days with a big orchestra and chorus of seventy people and Jeanette MacDonald and

Allan Jones and Robert Young and Ted Healy and Judy Garland and Sophie Tucker and plenty more.

There was also a dance routine with Eleanor Powell and George Murphy and a dozen Dave Gould dancing girls that was to work up to a terrific climax in which Buddy Ebsen came whirling into a solo tap dance break—only Mr. Ebsen came to the broadcast wearing sponge-soled golf shoes instead of taps, so on the air the big climax was sixteen measures of silence.

Also there was a Broadway Memories routine featuring Trixie Friganza, Irene Franklin, and Frankie Bailey, but when those old-timers came out on the stage and saw footlights they just naturally moved down to the apron and worked straight to the audience, completely ignoring the microphone, and the radio audience was treated to another hunk of confused silence. But anyhow we hit our stride before too many weeks and settled down into an hour of top glamour every Thursday night.

Sometimes one show alone would include Mickey Rooney, Joan Crawford, Bob Taylor, Clark Gable, Spencer Tracy, Frank Morgan, Freddie Bartholomew, Lionel Barrymore, Fannie Brice, Bob Montgomery, Luise Rainer, and Jimmy Stewart—but nevertheless, in the Mason City *Globe-Gazette* I would like you to know that the program was listed as "The Meredith Willson Hour."

Louis K. Sidney was now the head man of the *Good News* program, and did he come up with some lulus—maybe the greatest radio shows of all time. He had plenty of courage (still has) and he always tried for any progressive entertainment, and to heck with the rut and the sure-fire beaten path. We could use a few like him in radio now. Mr. Sidney is slightly busy nowadays, however, running M.G.M. for L. B. Mayer.

One day a couple of young writers brought him a piece of dramatic material for St. Patrick's Day. It was called *Fate Is Not Always a Lady* and Mr. Sidney decided to use it on the *Good News* show. The leading character sounded to him like Bob Montgomery, so he asked Bob to come in and talk it over.

Mr. Montgomery was very enthusiastic after seeing the material and suddenly Mr. Sidney said out of left field, "Bob, how'd you like to direct it as well as act in it?"

And Bob did and it was great and how did Mr. Sidney know that nine years later Bob Montgomery would be the most talked-of new director in the picture business?

Some General Foods (Maxwell House) big shots came out to Los Angeles about this time: Clarence Francis, Charlie Mortimer, and Ralph Starr Butler. It was pretty refreshing to see such important businessmen turn out to be normal, modest, hard-working human beings, the real American product, you might say, every one of them.

Arthur Lyons, the agent, gave a big party for them. I happened to walk by as Mr. Butler was saying to a beautiful blond vision, "Excuse me, I thought you were Virginia Verrill. She used to sing on our *Show Boat* program, you know."

"Oh yes, I know Virginia."

"Oh, do you live out here, ma'am?"

"Uhh—yes."

"And how do you like it?"

"Just fine."

"Pardon me, I'm Ralph Starr Butler. I'm afraid I didn't get your name."

"Myrna Loy."

About this time a young radio writer was hired by Mr. Sidney to produce the *Good News* show. We were doing an adaptation of *Marie Antoinette*, starring Norma Shearer, who, as everybody knows, is a very gracious lady. But many times picture people don't understand how important and inflexible seconds are in the radio business, and at the rehearsal she sort of did everything her own way, so this young producer didn't have a chance to get any kind of an accurate timing.

The unfortunate result was that we had to go on the air b'guess and b'God, and exactly sixty minutes later we went off the air right in the middle of the big scene in *Marie Antoinette*, and the young producer, of course, got fired the next day for not bringing the show out on time. If you didn't know it then, Miss Shearer, you do now, and it was all your fault, but don't feel too badly because he went to New York and as a last resort got on a CBS sustainer with a character he'd always wanted to play and the character was "Archie" and he was Ed Gardner.

22. WHEN I LEFT MASON CITY I SURE thought everybody would be different, and it gradually has come over me through the years that they aren't different at all. Too bad young ones don't believe that and have to find out for themselves. They'd just be that much smarter sooner.

I thought my folks invented that falsetto "yoo-hoo" out the back door at mealtime, but twenty years later I find out that mothers "yoo-hoo" for their kids all over the world.

Another thing. When you get to be my age you wish you'd been nicer to your folks. My father was always ready with the twenty-five cents a week spending money for my brother and me, and fifty cents extra every now and then for baseball games and special things like the fair, so why did we have to pull nasty little tricks on him besides? Like asking him for a nickel every time he'd be talking with a neighbor out in the front yard. We knew he'd always be kind of embarrassed to refuse in front of people, so usually we'd get away with it. Well, we didn't invent that either. That seems to be an instinctive little hunk of blackmail procedure, common to the kids of every generation.

There are some things, though, that you expect to be the same all over the world and that turn out different; simple things like the drumbeat in the parade. Did you ever stop to realize that the American basic drumbeat we use for our parade rhythms isn't heard in any other country? I mean that old bass drumbeat:

> Boom
> Boom
> Boom boom boom

Every country has its own basic parade beat, and most of them don't even remotely resemble ours.

Then there is the matter of the rooster. I suppose you think that children all over the world say "cock-a-doodle-do." Well, if you don't think so, you are pretty smart because the Russian kids saw "koo-ka reh-koooo," Spanish kids say "ki-kiri-kiii," the Dutch kids say "ku-kele-ku," the French kids say "co-co-ri-co," the little native kids from Africa say "ri-ki-ri-ki-ri-ki."

And almost every place when they sing about a big bell it's always "ding-dong," the same as here, but a little bell is something else again. We say "ting-a-ling," in Mexico they say "tilin-tilin," and in Russia they say "deen-deen-deen."

But for the most part, as I started to say, kids and their folks are pretty much the same all over the world. Abe Meyer's mama in Flushing and my mama in Mason City—both probably had the same way of holding the pillow under their chin when they wanted to put on the clean pillow slip. They both probably looked through the bookcase with the same anxiety every time a neighbor kid had a birthday party, looking to find a book that was almost new, so you'd have a present to take. And probably both, with their patient fingers, tried to erase the peanut-butter stains or the herring stains from the pages, and to cut a new jacket for this book out of some shiny paper tucked away in the sideboard. "It's just the thing!" she would say in Flushing or Mason City, trying to reassure you that your gift wouldn't be shoddy at all but gleaming and special.

And I guess everybody goes through the growing-up period where his vocabulary changes, and he's ashamed of his folks because they say yard for lawn and sofa for chesterfield and supper instead of dinner, sociable for charming, picture show for theater.

The first time I came home after living in New York I probably said things like "Rivahside

Drive," "Plahza Hotel," and "I mean to say" before and after every remark. And I can hear my friend Abe, after his first trip to the Golden West, rushing into his Flushing parlor and slapping his mom on the back with a hearty "Hi ho thar, podner, whadaya got fer chow?" But Long Island or Iowa, we never looked foolish to Mama.

23. WE FINISHED UP THE FIRST
Good News season in a blaze of glory, splitting
a forty rating just about fifty-fifty with our oppo-
sition, Major Bowes. The plan was to go off the
air for the summer, so I thought, If I'm ever
going to get to Europe I'd better go.

We crossed in about six days, and Plymouth
looked just like it did in the history books. We
did the usual sight-seeing in London—the Wax
Museum and everything—and then took a plane
for Paris and ran into Abel Green, the editor of
Variety, which was just fine, and also good luck
because Mr. Green ran *Variety's* Paris office some
years before and sure did know his way around
Paris.

One day we took a drive to Versailles and on
the way we passed through a sleepy little village
which looked completely deserted and a thousand
years old. Mr. Green bet me a franc that he could
pick out any door along the street and it would
turn out to be a place where we could buy an

American coke. I took the bet and we stopped the car and opened the first door we saw. It led into a courtyard and there sat Erich von Stroheim, posing with studied nonchalance in faultless white flannels, with a great Dane on one side and a beautiful blond secretary on the other—just in case somebody should walk in, I guess, yet so far as we knew there wasn't anyone within forty miles of there. Herr von Stroheim rose and clicked his heels. Across his face there brushed a slight trace of satisfaction that this charming tableaux hadn't been wasted on an empty garden. Aside from that, however, he was completely in character—the implacable Prussian officer impeccably relaxing between wars. A waiter appeared. I had a cup of tea and one lump. For Mr. Green, an American coke and of course one franc—my franc. We refreshed ourselves, expressed our thanks, and quietly slipped out as Le Grand Illusion automatically resumed his upstage situation between his lovely Scandinavians—the beautiful blond secretary and the gorgeous great Dane. Back in London, the BBC invited me to see a television broadcast, which was pretty exciting for the first thirty seconds while you were saying to yourself, My, my! How can they possibly send pictures through the air like that? But beginning with the next thirty seconds and thereafter it was simply a boring short subject on a home movie set, and I may be dumb but I still think that television will be only as successful as the quality of entertainment they give you on that little screen.

A real nice man named Fred Bates showed me around and invited me to conduct a broadcast with the BBC orchestra, but in the meantime a cold I had picked up flying back from Paris got worse and made me beg off the broadcast on account of my ears were stopped up and, although I felt completely okay, I wouldn't have been able to tell an A from an A flat, or muted brass from open, and naturally, wanting to put my best foot forward, I simply sent word that I was ill and couldn't do the broadcast. That evening I was having cocktails in the hotel when two very embarrassing things happened simultaneously, (1) Mr. Fred BBC Bates walked in, giving me a somewhat quizzical, not to say restrained, greeting just as (2) the proprietor turned on the radio which said, "The broadcawst you will now hehya is seated in international good will, occasioned as it is by the circmstnce of a tempry disorder affecting the health of the Ameddican conductor, Mr. Mededith Willson of the NBC to whom, on his couch of pain, the subsequent items of this program are dedicated." I should have been able to explain to Mr. Bates, but I just turned red, left a half crown and a half-finished martini on my couch of pain, and left.

To get my mind off this unhappy turn of events, I stopped in at a small antique shop on King's Road to inquire about an old tortoise-shell snuff-box I saw in the window.

This shop was fitted in under the stairway of the adjoining building and was only maybe four by six feet. Two alpaca gentlemen were the proprietors, it seemed—both well over seventy, but regardless of the half century they must have spent together under those stairs, they still addressed each other as "Oh, Mr. Hezlitt"—"Coming, Mr. Hotchkiss."

This charming formality was in noticeable contrast to my experience at the Dorchester House later that night when suddenly the orchestra started a tune I didn't know and everybody on the dance floor lined up in twos and started promenading and hitting their knees all at the same time, including the Duke and Duchess of Kent, who were particularly energetic about crying, "Hoy," which they all did every once in a while. Everybody had that serious, English, this-is-a-job-and-let's-get-it-over-with look about them, and it turned out to be the "Lambeth Walk," and I brought the music back home with me to be the first to do it on the *Good News* program that fall. But I'm sorry to say at least four other orchestra leaders beat me to it.

I spent my last day in Europe with the Abel

Greens at the race track, and during the afternoon we ran into Darryl Zanuck, who was really turned out like a perfect English gentleman: pearl-gray bowler, gray cutaway, pin-striped trousers, fawn-colored spats, binoculars suspended around his neck. A young friend of Mr. Green's named Forrest joined us and asked to be introduced to Mr. Zanuck, whom he had heard about and admired greatly.

Mr. Green said, "Mr. Zanuck—meet Mr. Forrest," and out of the great man—out of this faultlessly attired "Oxfordian"—came that Wahoo, Nebraska, twang, "Har ya, Forst? Glada meetcha."

Mr. Forrest acknowledged the introduction with considerable consternation apparent on his open face and, turning to me, he whispered, "Bad dubbing job."

24. THE "GOOD NEWS" SERIES STARTED
up again in September, and one day Mr. Sidney
bought a hunk of script from George Kaufman
called *If Men Played Bridge as Women Do*. It
was a very funny piece of business and was all set
for the show that week. It called for four men,
but somebody miscounted or something, and when
they started to rehearse it the only actors on the
show that week were Robert Taylor and Spencer
Tracy and Hanley Stafford (who had been hired
to play Daddy to Fannie Brice's Baby Snooks).
So out of desperation they gave the part with the
fewest lines to me, and the part with fewest lines
turned out to be the funniest and we did a new
skit about *If Men Do as Women Do* every week
the rest of that year, and I'll be John Brown if
I wasn't on my way to becoming a perfectly practi-
cal radio stooge.

Albert Coates was then conducting the Los
Angeles Philharmonic and I was invited to lunch

to meet him. There were mostly musicians at this lunch, who were, as usual, exchanging musicians' stories—you know—all about Liszt and Hans von Bülow and Richard Strauss.

Everybody had heard everybody else's stories, but everybody laughed politely anyway, and then Mr. Coates said, "Here's one about Dr. Nikisch and one of your famous Ameddican orchestras, the Boston Symphony. The doctor needed a new first trombone player and picked out a young man with a fine technique but no orchestra experience. At the first rehearsal Nikisch said, 'Gentlemen, the opening work on the program is the Tschaikowsky 'Sixth.' You all know it, so just turn it over—that is'—and he thought of his new first trombone—'I *think* you all know it. You—the new first trombone—you know the 'Sixth' Tschaikowsky of course?' The young man cleared his throat and very clearly and unmistakably said, 'No sir.' The orchestra tittered and Nikisch said, 'Well, you've at least heard it, haven't you?' The young man said, 'No sir.' And Nikisch was so taken aback that all he could think of to say was, 'I hope you enjoy it!' "

Well, everybody laughed moderately and then I said, "Mr. Coates, that's pretty funny, but you have some of the details wrong. First of all it wasn't Nikisch—it was Van Hoogstraten, and it wasn't the Boston Symphony—it was the New

York Philharmonic—it wasn't the 'Sixth' Tschaikowsky—it was the 'Leonore Overture' by Beethoven, and it wasn't a trombone player at all, it was a flute player. In fact, it was me!"

Mr. Coates seemed to enjoy this whole exchange hugely, and we started visiting, and I got up the nerve to ask him if he would care to play my first symphony at any time in the near future, and he said, "I'd rather play your second symphony," and I said, "I haven't written any second symphony," and he said, "Exactly."

However, I preferred to take the kindlier interpretation of his remark, so I immediately started writing a second symphony. It was about the missions of California, and when I finished it Mr. Coates said, "Bully, I'll play it." He did, in my lucky month of April, and all my friends said they liked the new symphony just fine. In fact, Mr. Coates said, "I understand that in addition to composing you do something on the wireless. I feel it my djewty to keep up with all the modern Ameddican activities. When is your broadcawst and may I attend?"

Naturally I was delighted and invited Mr. Coates to attend the Maxwell House show on the Thursday following the performance of my symphony. He stayed just long enough to see me put down the baton, walk to the microphone with a piece of celery in each hand and an old light bulb between my teeth, and engage in a bit of stooge dialogue with Frank Morgan, which ended, as usual, with Mr. Morgan saying, "Get out of my sight, you bucolic nincompoop, you country bumpkin, you—you—you peasant!"

Mr. Coates rose to his feet and quietly left the studio, and I have never laid eyes on him since.

Meanwhile a man phoned my friend, Mr. Abe Meyer (who was a well-known agent in the picture business by this time), and this man said he had heard my symphony and did Mr. Meyer know if I would like to write the music for a new Charlie Chaplin picture called *The Great Dictator*, and Mr. Meyer said, "I'll ask him. Who's speaking, please?" and he said, "Charlie Chaplin."

I can't say I see eye to eye with Mr. Chaplin about a lot of things, including his politics, and I think he is a very selfish and in many ways inconsiderate man, but I also think he is a great artist and I will certainly say that it was a real pleasure to watch him day after day and see him tick.

I've seen him take a sound track and cut it all up and paste it back together and come up with some of the dangedest effects you ever heard— effects a composer would never think of. Don't kid yourself about that one. He would have been great at anything—music, law, ballet dancing, or painting—house, sign, or portrait. I got the screen credit for *The Great Dictator* music score, but the best parts of it were all Charlie's ideas, like using the *Lohengrin* "Prelude" in the famous balloon-dance scene.

The scene in the barbershop where Chaplin shaved a customer to the strains of Brahms's "Hungarian Dance Number Five" was all made before I ever came on the lot. They had played a phonograph record as they photographed Mr. Chaplin doing the shaving to the tempo of the music. For the finished picture, of course, it was my job to record the music with a big orchestra, synchronized to Mr. Chaplin's movements in the picture. In other words, the original scene was made with Mr. Chaplin fitting his movements to the music of a phonograph. Now it was necessary for me to fit the music of my orchestra to his movements. We planned to do it very painstakingly, eight measures or maybe even less at a time, taking a couple of weeks to do the job.

We started early one Monday morning and decided to run the whole scene once with the orchestra to give us an over-all idea, and Mr. Chaplin said, "We may as well record it while we're at it—film is cheap and we might get a few measures to save." So we let 'er roll and at the end of the scene Mr. Chaplin fell flat on his face on the sound stage, yelling, "That's it, that's it!" And sure enough, by dumb luck we had managed to catch every movement, and that was the first and only "take" made of that scene, the one used in the finished picture.

I sure did enjoy lunching with Mr. Chaplin, which happened every day for ten weeks in his bungalow on the lot. Believe me, I learned something about humor—timing and all that.

He kept us laughing through every lunch, day after day, and never told a single joke—only true experiences or things he had observed during the morning. He is a real genius, I guess, though he does some awfully strange things for a genius, like not becoming a citizen. I read his explanation of that in the paper. He said he was an international citizen. Didn't belong to any one country. And that remark hit me like a nightmare. Imagine standing in the middle of the world like in a Dali painting as an international citizen. Suddenly this made me remember one of those things we used to rattle off in grammar school: "Breathes there a man with soul so dead, who never to himself hath said . . ." And right then those old lines practically drowned me in goose-pimples, and pride, and purpose, and obligation, and gratitude. The goose-pimples quieted down, but those other things will never leave me from here on out. So thank you very much, Mr. Chaplin, for a real lesson in patriotism.

$25.$ I DID QUITE A LITTLE COMPOSING
that year, and in addition to finishing my second
symphony and *The Great Dictator* score, I wrote a
symphonic poem, "The Jervis Bay," and a popular
song called "You and I."

I wrote the words for this song as well as the
music and it turned out to be the only song lyric
in captivity that is just one sentence long. It goes
like this: "Darling, you and I know the reason
why a summer sky is blue, and we know why birds
in the trees sing melodies too, and why love will
grow from the first 'hello' until the last 'good-
by,' so to sweet romance there is just one answer:
You and I."

Jack Robbins is a music-publisher friend of
mine, often referred to as the Bonaparte of Tin
Pan Alley, also the Little Napoleon, also many
other things by rival publishers—but what I
wanted to say was, Mr. Robbins said he'd like to
publish "You and I," but there happened to be

an ASCAP fight on at that time, which I won't explain because if you're a member of ASCAP you'll remember the fight, and if you're not you won't be at all interested. And because of this fight Mr. Robbins wasn't publishing any songs just then, but he advised me to publish it myself, which I did.

The printer sent me the first edition and the back cover was blank and I thought it looked amateurish because every professional song always has eight bars or so of several other songs being advertised there on the back, so I scribbled out eight measures to put on the back cover, and he wired back, "Everybody here likes this new song better than 'You and I.' Where's the rest of it?"

And that's how I happened to write a song called "Two in Love," and both "You and I" and "Two in Love" got on the Hit Parade at the same time, which I thought was slightly ironic, or poetic justice, or sump'n, in view of the fact that I invented the Hit Parade.

If you like coincidences, by the way, there are two that happened to me which chronologically belong more or less in here somewhere. The theme for the slow movement of my Mission Symphony is called "San Juan Bautista," and it goes like this:

Next, I started working on the scherzo move-ment and went to visit San Juan Capistrano, be-cause this scherzo was to be about the Capistrano Mission. I asked two very sweet sisters at the mis-sion if there was any characteristic music that had been handed down from the eighteenth-century days of Father Junípero Serra, the founder of the missions—a great, great man whose life should be taught in all the public schools. They said there was one typical chant handed down from those times, and they gave it to me. In fact, Sister Agnes wrote it out right then.

I really thought I was seeing things when I looked at the music:

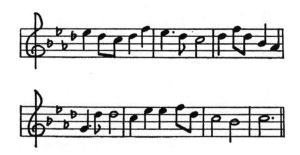

As you see, this theme and the one I had already written months before fit contrapuntally together like a glove:

and I was in the goose-pimple department again.

The other coincidence has to do with an armed British freighter by the name of *Jervis Bay*, which got sunk while saving a thirty-eight-ship convoy from a German pocket battleship. It hit me as one of the bravest actions I had ever heard about and inspired me to try my hand at a symphonic poem for orchestra. That was in November, and I just had it finished in January when my friend, Mr. Louis K. Sidney, phoned about the music for a Greek War Relief radio program we were doing together at Grauman's Chinese Theatre. He told me he was sending over a piece of special material Gene Fowler had written for Ronald Colman to read on the program, which would need quite an elaborate musical score.

The material turned out to be a beautiful prose poem called *The Jervis Bay Goes Down* and, with practically no changes at all, it—and the symphonic piece I had already written—fit like they were made for each other. But the nice thing was that Gene Fowler and Ronald Colman became my friends and they are very remarkable men and two of the "good guys" besides. Also, Monsieur Monteux put my original orchestra version of "The Jervis Bay" on one of his April concerts with the San Francisco Symphony in the beautiful San Francisco Opera House.

After the concert, as I started out of the stage door, a man was waiting for me and handed me a big transcription recording. I said, "What is this?" and the man said, "Your friends in the engineering department over at NBC thought you would like a recording of your new composition, so they made it for you and here it is," and I said, "How could this be? This concert wasn't even broadcast, so how could they pick it up to record?" And the man said, "That's easy—Jim Summers in the control room back at the studio just opened up the line from the Opera House to NBC's recording department, and when the lights went down for your number one of the boys sneaked down the aisle with the microphone and plugged 'er in."

Now how nice can people be?

26. ALONG ABOUT THIS TIME A FELLO named Sam Goldwyn was producing a picture called *The Little Foxes*, and just because I *didn't* want to do the music for it he wanted me to, which is characteristic of Hollywood and Mr. Goldwyn. In fact, I guess, to some extent it's human nature.

Anyhow. I got my gang together and we moved in on the Goldwyn studio.

It has been said that Mr. Goldwyn's press agents make up all those Goldwynisms like: "Include me out," and "I can tell you in just two words: im-possible." All I know is, I was in his office one day when his secretary came in and said, "Mr. Goldwyn, the filing cabinets are full of so much correspondence that I have no room for anything. Will you allow me to sort out the old letters and burn them?"

Mr. Goldwyn said, "Of course, I wish you would—but be sure to keep copies."

Well, I had written a theme for *The Little Foxes* which I wasn't any too sure of, so I thought I'd better try it out with a small orchestra. Also, I wanted to try out a new arranger, so I gave the theme to this man and told him I only wanted it arranged for an orchestra of eleven men—no cello.

He phoned me in the middle of the night, saying, "This theme needs a cello badly. Please change your mind. I would give ten years off Hitler's life for just one cello."

Now I thought this was a pretty funny remark at the time and when I bumped into Mr. Goldwyn the next day walking across the lot with the very fine director of the picture, Willie Wyler, I thought I would tell the great man the story. I gave the punch line everything I had and got no reaction at all from Mr. Goldwyn. He simply said, "If that man can't arrange a simple piece for you without a cello, he's too expensive. Get rid of him."

We finished the picture and went to the sneak preview, which with Mr. Goldwyn is an experience. He dies a thousand deaths and paces up and down in front of the theater, raving at everybody except the cameraman, Gregg Toland, who is wise to this trying procedure and always stays home and Mr. Toland somehow usually wins the Academy awards anyway. So does Mr. Goldwyn, come to think of it.

Of course the picture was a great deal too long —they always are—and my best music got left on the cutting-room floor—it always does—but outside of that, it was an interesting experience which, like the Army, I am glad to have behind me.

I wrote a spiritual for that picture called "Never Feel Too Weary to Pray," which got practically cut out of the picture, except in the main title, but it came in handy later, as I will now recount to you.

I had been arguing and arguing with Willie Wyler, the director, about the finish of the picture. It was none of my business, but the character played by Bette Davis had killed her husband, stolen from everybody, including her own brothers, and was so obnoxious that her own daughter finally told her off and left her flat— and I'm just corny enough to want such a character to get her comeuppance good and plenty, retribution and all like that. Instead, the picture finished on Bette with an extremely hateful look on her face as she watched her daughter going off down the street in the rain and out of her life, but on her face was no indication that she was sorry to see her own child leave her, or that she had any conscience whatever about any of the awful things she had done.

I asked Willie, "She doesn't get away with it, does she?" And Willie said, "Sure she does. She's got the money. She's rid of her husband. And she goes to Chicago and lives off the fat of the land the rest of her life."

I said, "What about retribution—her just deserts and everything?"

He said, "She was just a selfish, evil woman who was clever and had no conscience and no regrets and nobody ever caught up with her and that's all there is to it."

Well, I hollered and screamed that there's always got to be justice and she should at least look a little frightened or disturbed in that last scene of the picture, but Willie laughed at me and said, "Too late—the picture is shot—it's done—it's over and finished and I wouldn't change it even if I could, which I wouldn't."

But I double-crossed you, Willie Wyler, in case you never realized it. That spiritual, "Never Feel Too Weary to Pray," has a middle part that goes like this:

> Oh Lord, sound the trump of the Judgment,
> Oh Lord, hurry on to that day!

So for the end title music I used a chorus of voices, and just as the shot of Bette Davis's face was fading into THE END I started the voices singing those words. The only trouble was that at practically every theater they go immediately into the newsreel and seldom stay with the feature through the end title, unless it's the last showing at midnight, and frequently not then either, on account of the projectionist is in a hurry to get home. But anyhow—my Iowa conscience felt better.

27. IF YOU'RE INTERESTED IN VIRTUES like modesty, all-around gentlemanliness, and thoroughbred behavior, you'll usually find them in the person who is the best in his line. Like a personality I knew whose nickname was Bob.

He was known all over the world as 'way head and shoulders The Best in his line. He never actually did his stuff in America, yet he was idolized and respected here just the same as he was at home. I met him once and, jeepers, what a Natural—warm, tolerant, understanding, calm, simple, but what an aristocrat.

A man with his qualities might pull this world out of a few of the holes we've gotten into. Unfortunately, however, I'm not talking about a man. I'm talking about a big chestnut horse named Phar Lap.

Anybody who is real big and who knows what he's doing and has his finger on his number all the time is usually a "good guy" like Phar Lap was. Phar Lap, by the way, is a Siamese name and means "Wink of the Sky"—in other words, Lightning—and he sure was, too. Came in first in every start, but modest and all. Let the others kick up at the barrier and carry on so fancy. That's just because they're not real sure of themselves. They don't know what they're doing.

You know, the farther away I get from Mason City by the calendar, the faster I seem to be coming back to the old values and things we used to take for granted back home—like not taking things for granted. Everybody back home took for granted that certain things were just naturally worth while, like making jelly and tomato preserves in the summertime so you'd have them for later on in the winter. But when you busted through that paraffin in December or January to enjoy that jelly you never forgot for a minute how Mama worked in August—filling the cheesecloth bag with the crab apples, twisting it around the faucet in the sink, twisting and twisting till the jelly juice got all squeezed out.

But I was saying about it's real good to know what you're doing. If you don't, it makes a lot of sense to quit it and get to doing something that feels more comfortable to you.

Some kids in our manual-training class couldn't drive a nail straight—like me. I fussed around for months trying to make a pair of book ends (cloverleaf pattern). Now you've never seen anything as awkward in your whole born days as (1) me working on those book ends and (2) those book ends after I finished them. They wobbled a couple of times on the table next to the hall tree and fell down and never did get up again.

It's just lucky for the book-end people that I took up the flute. Oh, sure, I took up the drums first. Everybody takes up the drums. But I was just as awkward with the drums as I was with the book ends, only I didn't have brains enough to recognize it because the drums were pretty fascinating, and besides, you got to march in the W.C.T.U. parade and all. Mama was the one who knew I didn't seem to be taking to those drumsticks any too well, so she put the flute idea into my head.

All I wanted to say was it's good to think about Mason City and remember summer's apple squeezing when you're enjoying winter's jelly, and also your whole life is more enjoyable when you work at things you feel comfortable doing instead of awkward.

Like one day when I went to get a haircut on a Saturday without an appointment and naturally found all the barbers tied up except Harry, the owner of the shop, who is a remarkable businessman that everybody knows out here and also likes, and Harry said, "I've got an extra chair because one of my barbers is sick and if you don't mind my stopping frequently to handle the cash register, because my cashier is sick too, I'll cut your hair myself."

Well, all the barbers in that shop are just great, but I've never in my whole born days been worked on by such a master as this Harry. Can't explain the difference, but everything he did was just full of character, that's all, and when I left I said, "Harry, now I know why you own your own business."

Harry laughed and he said, "Oh, I can cut hair, I guess, but it doesn't hurt to be pleasant too," and he told me about the night he went to the Trocadero for dinner. There was Harry Cohn, head of Columbia Pictures, and across the room at another table a producer named Perlberg, who was having a real "drop-dead" feud with Mr. Cohn about something in the picture business.

My friend Harry, the barbershop proprietor, noticed Mr. Perlberg was having a birthday celebration, so he asked the waiter to send a bottle of champagne over to the table with his compliments. The producer was much pleased and said, "Who sent it?" and the waiter said, "Harry." And Mr. P. naturally thought he meant Harry Cohn and he immediately rushed up to the orchestra leader, and a few minutes later the musicians

183

struck up with "Harry Cohn's a jolly good fellow, Harry Cohn's a jolly good fellow," and in
thirty seconds Mr. Cohn and Mr. Perlberg had
their arms around each other and the feud was
over. Isn't that interesting?

28. AFTER THREE PLEASANT YEARS MAX-
well House and M.G.M. decided to go their sep-
arate ways. So everybody shook hands all around,
nostalgically happy—happy about a fine radio
series, and nostalgic because this series was disap-
pearing into the limbo—and Maxwell House gave
birth to the Frank Morgan-Fannie Brice show
which starred Robert Young as emcee, and again I
went along with the deal.

We used to go out to the Youngs' ranch on
Sunday where Mr. and Mrs. Young sure threw
some nice informal meals. Never forget when they
went to Europe and came back with a wonderful story about being entertained in London by
Lord Somebody. It was an intimate dinner with
only His Lordship and Her Ladyship and Mr. and
Mrs. Young.

At the end of the dinner the host, with a great
deal of ceremony, brought up from the cellar the
last of the Napoleon brandy which had been
handed down in his family—*real* Napoleon

brandy, not the two-dollars-a-drink stuff that was made in the town where the grandson of the man who lived across the street from the nephew of the guy who used to exchange stories with Napoleon's wine-cellar keeper lived. In other words, this was *real Napoleon brandy* and His Lordship had been pointing this out to Mr. Young while Her Ladyship and Mrs. Young were going yadata-yadata-yadata over in the corner.

Well, you may know Mr. Young was pretty impressed and stood breathlessly by while the host himself squeezed out the very last drop into four huge brandy snifters and carried the first one over to Mrs. Young.

"What's this?" she said over her shoulder.

"Dear," said Mr. Young in awe-stricken tones, "it's Napoleon brandy."

"Oh, fine," Mrs. Young said. "Plenty of soda and not too much ice."

If this had been in the funnies the last picture would have shown His Lordship flat on his back with his remarks ballooning out of his mouth somewhat as follows: "OW—OW—OW—OW." At any rate, conversation definitely waned and Mr. and Mrs. Young left very shortly after that and were given a somewhat formal, not to say cool, "Good night."

Mrs. Young might have come from Iowa, not being impressed with Napoleon brandy, I mean.

Our state was prohibition long before the first World War, and Mason City was *positively* prohibition clear back to the days when it was Owens Grove, which was practically a present from the United States to my grandfather, Alonzo Willson, by way of a homestead at $1.25 an acre.

We used to go out to my grandfather's farm in the summer to pick those little round, sweet, dark red plums, and we'd always hammer open the seeds, but I don't know why because that little nut inside tasted awful. We also used to open peach stones, and when I was in high school I firmly believed that the almond people watered the almonds with the nuts out of peach stones, which seems kind of silly, impractical, and rather uneconomical to me now.

We also went to Grampa's for black walnuts and the stains stayed on your hands till sumac time in the fall. If you hear people call that "shoomac" they are from Iowa because that's what we call it. The kids all carried armfuls of it to the teacher in September—also violets in the spring.

Grampa raised one family of five children back in New York. Their names were Aunt Emma, Aunt Alice, Uncle B.B., Uncle Bruce, and Aunt Norie. They all grew up and got married, so Grampa and Gramma Willson decided they would ox-team it to Ioway and look into the homestead department. They did, and settled in

Owens Grove and raised another family: Aunt Mae, Aunt Gertrude, and Papa, and that's how it happened that Papa had a sister old enough to be his mother and I've got an aunt pushing a hundred. She's my aunt Alice and she lives in Bushton, Kansas, and the last time I saw her she was driving her own car, eating with her own teeth, reading with her own eyes, and writing a gossip column for the local paper. Her married name is Shonyo and nobody ever heard of that name before.

When I was trouping with Sousa it used to be a hobby of mine to look in all the phone books in all the different towns hunting for the name of Shonyo, but I never found one. I asked my aunt Alice about this and she answered me thusly: It seems her husband got shot through the mouth in the Battle of Gettysburg with a musket ball. His papers were all destroyed when they found him on the battlefield and took him to an Army hospital. When he came to they asked him what his name was and he said "Shonyo" and they wrote it down. Of course that isn't what he said at all. What he said was "Shannon"—plain old Irish Shannon—but shoot yourself through the mouth with a musket ball and try to say "Shannon" and it will come out "Shonyo" every time. By that time he was being mustered out, and all his Army papers described him as Shonyo, and if you've ever been in the Army, you know it's much easier to change your name than it is to get the Army to change anything. So I have an aunt named Aunt Alice Shonyo.

But to get back to the subject of prohibition in Mason City, I was very surprised to find out from my cousin Phil, who is now a remarkable public-relations man in New York, also a playwright with a nose for such things, that a former principal of the Mason City grade schools had wine with practically every meal—dandelion wine from his own cellar—and I had grown up and left Mason City believing that nobody there ever even tasted alcohol, not counting the time that Ed White, down at the butcher shop, gave Papa a bottle of beer. Papa came home and marched into the kitchen with a very determined jaw and that beer, also fifteen cents' worth of brick cheese, and Mama turned pale and we children huddled breathlessly under the sink.

But Papa had made his decision. There's gotta be beer and cheese in the life of every man at least once. He opened the big drawer in the cupboard, took out the bread knife and got the big loaf out of the breadbox, made a cheese sandwich for himself and opened the beer and drank it out of the bottle, hating every swallow, I'm sure, but the die was cast. He saw his challenge to manhood and he accepted it.

Supper came and went in silence. We were sure Papa was drunk. He changed the mantle in the gas light that night, but his hand didn't seem to us at all steady as he slipped the new mantle on and adjusted the light with the delicate little chains hanging down. He sat in his big brown rocker and read us our chapter of *The Last of the Mohicans*, but his voice sure sounded funny, we thought, and once he said "Chingachook" instead of "Chingachgook." Mama, of course, hadn't spoken a single word since the tragedy. We went up to bed but not to sleep.

Then it happened. Stumbling and smashing noises as the kitchen stool fell over and something crashed against the cellar door. The stove lids rattled and we knew Papa was having delirium tremens. The back door flew open—then the entry door—and the winter night blew through the house, making the hall curtains, the reed ones with the eucalyptus seeds, thrash weirdly, noisily.

We buried our heads under the covers and said thirty or forty "Now-I-lay-me's," and morning finally came. I was still so scared I forgot to fight with my brother Cedric about closing the window, and I shivered across the floor and closed it without thinking, scraping my initials in the white frost down the pane automatically with my fingernails.

Papa always made the buckwheat cakes when

we had them for breakfast, and this morning he was up before anybody and had them made and on the table. (He also made the oyster stew at night whenever we had it, in the big white breakfast food bowls—the Egg-O-See bowls. I hated the oysters but I loved the butter floating in the stew and the small round oyster crackers.)

Anyway, Papa said, "Good morning," and Mama said, "John, what was that noise last night?" and Papa said, "Why, I finally caught that rat that's been eating the cheese out of the trap. Killed him with the broom and threw him out on the ash heap."

The Demon Rum never entered our lives again, although nowadays I do accept an occasional glass of beer.

29. POINTS OF VIEW CHANGE, DON'T
they? I already mentioned that I used to think
"doily" was a naughty word. Used to mix it up with
"diaper," I guess, which, of course, nobody would
ever say in front of anybody. Well, only last week
I saw a laundry service ad in the Los Annelus
Times—"Rock-A-Dry-Baby"—and I must say I
was taken even farther apace by the ad for a new
kind of men's shorts with a print design of big red
ants, and these new shorts have a name. They are
called ANTSY-PANTS.

Everybody has earth-shaking ideas like that
sooner or later. Grow mushrooms in the cellar!
Plant black walnut saplings in the back yard and
raise a grove of airplane struts and gun butts!

I had two earth shakers. The first was to paint
successive-action pictures one after the other in
the tunnel of the New York subway—pictures like
those black-and-white drawings in the little books
you used to flip past your eye. The successive-

192

action drawings made it look like moving pictures, remember? Well, the principle would be the same in the tunnel of the subway, only instead of flipping the pictures past your eye with your thumb, the subway train would flip you (and your eye) past the pictures.

The other one was to make a breakfast food, sort of like loose shredded wheat chopped up, and call it "Short Shrift."

In San Francisco one day a friend of mine dropped in, which surprised me at the time because he lived in New York. He was carrying with him a banged-up, scrawny, suspicious-looking ladies' traveling hatbox which he cautiously and lovingly laid on the desk.

Out of his overcoat pocket he took a can of fruit salad and a can opener. Then out of the hatbox he took a weird-looking contraption, all haywired together, and plugged it into the wall socket. As this device started going hunkacha-hunkacha-hunkacha, he opened the fruit salad, dumped it into the contraption for about thirty seconds, pulled out the plug, poured what used to be fruit salad into a tumbler he got from his inside pocket, and said, "Drink this."

Yes—everybody gets earth-shaking ideas sooner or later, the only difference is that this fellow's earth shaker worked. His name is Fred Waring and the contraption is now called the Waring Mixer.

Fred Waring is also distinguished for his willingness to go to hellangone just for a gag. We got into a polite argument the day he unveiled his mixer about the relative carrying power of high and low frequencies. I reminded him that when a parade was approaching from far off, the first thing you heard was the piccolo. He thanked me for reminding him of this but pleasantly insisted that even before you heard the sounds of the piccolo you always heard the thud of the bass drum.

The upshot of this intellectual, not to say cultural, discussion was a pre-dawn rendezvous that took us out into San Francisco Bay, where we dodged ferryboats and tugs and barges for an hour as we rowed over to what is now Treasure Island. For the rest of the morning we marched over that wave-splattered, wind-beaten rock, trilling and thumping our respective instruments like two thirds of the Spirit of '76, trying to prove which sound carried the farthest to a pretty disgusted committee who strained their ears from the clock tower on top of the Ferry Building back on the mainland, and of course heard nothing at all but the usual comings and goings of the early-morning bay traffic.

I guess Fred was eclipsed, though, in the matter

of "anything for a gag" by one Phil Rapp, a talented little man who wrote the Morgan-Brice Maxwell House program and often referred to Mr. Morgan and Miss Brice as "figments of his imagination."

After each show Al Kaye, the producer, always called this fine writer on the phone to ask how the show came over, as Mr. Rapp preferred to listen to it at home rather than at the studio.

One week we really had a stinker. Mr. Morgan may have lost count of his juleps before going on the air and taken too many or too few, and Miss Brice's timing may have been off, and the script may have been a little hungry—but whatever it was, the show laid a large egg. The producer called Phil as usual, heard the phone ring just once, then heard the receiver being taken off the hook. Nobody said hello or anything, and the next thing he heard was a revolver shot and that was the end of the conversation, and that's going a long way for a gag, but funny, don't you think? And if you're thinking it would have been even funnier if Mr. Rapp had really shot himself, I hope you don't mean it unkindly.

30. DURING OUR '40–'41 SEASON BENE-
fits had become more and more frequent. Hardly a
week went by without a special Red Cross broadcast or Bundles for Britain or Greek Relief or Russian Relief. And then one Sunday morning, wham!
we were at war, so everybody immediately began to
worry about how he could best serve his country
and we all bought black-out curtains and went to
the firehouse to see a demonstration of how to
put out a magnesium bomb with a stirrup pump.

I looked at my stirrup pump just the other day
and thought how quickly it became a completely
useless, outdated war relic along with the blunder-
buss and crossbows of other wars.

Anyway, I thought probably the best thing I
could do was to try to be an asset in mufti rather
than a liability in uniform, and there certainly
were bound to be a lot of bond drives on the radio
and special songs to be written that somebody
would have to write. So I decided not to join up,

and whadayaknow, the first thing I knew, I got a call from Washington, D.C., from the Office of Defense Transportation.

The man said, "We need a song for the civilian truck drivers, something to show them how important their job is here at home. Tell 'em to watch their tires, don't be a soft-shoe slob, don't be a clutch jockey, don't be a road hog. Why, Mr. Willson, if you can get all those things into a song it'll be another 'Ol' Man River'!"

Slightly dazed but with tremendous fervor, I started to work and knocked out a little dilly—but not exactly a second "Ol' Man River"—called "My Ten-Ton Baby and Me." Sent this off in the next morning air-mail with the music and three months later received a copy of the *Truck Drivers' Journal*, which reprinted the song somewhere in the back, and that's all that ever happened to that one.

However, I'm not easily discouraged, and when *This Is the Army* made such a hit I was ready with a whole musical comedy for the Navy, complete with music, lyrics, book, and star (I had shown it to Walter Huston and he said, "Let's go"). I rushed down to Spring Street to see Captain Jack Bolton and Commander Adolph Zukor, who were very interested, and I could practically hear the overture and see the curtain rise on Act I, except that two days later they phoned to tell me that the

Navy had decided not to have any show at all. The mere fact that the Army had had a show was sufficient to convince the Navy that it was a bad idea.

But meanwhile Marco Wolfe, who is half of Fanchon and Marco, called and said he needed special material and songs for USO units that were going out all the time and did I have anything, and I said you bet and sat right down and wrote a thing called "Gangway, You Rats, Gangway." I wrote eight or ten different sets of lyrics and went down to the Paramount and rushed backstage to play the song for Mr. Wolfe, and he thought it was just fine, and so did quite a lot of acts who were sitting around listening. I had a bunch of mimeographed copies, so I passed them out and we all sat around singing "Gangway, You Rats, Gangway," and then I went home just in time to get a call from a WAC captain who said they needed a song badly for the WAC. So I said I'm your boy and knocked out a thing called "Yankee Doodle Girl."

Sent it off in the next mail and received word from WAC headquarters only a few days later, "Don't get any ideas about your WAC song becoming official. We already have a WAC song by a lieutenant of the corps, copy enclosed."

Well, I was a little discouraged by this time, but just then the phone rang and it's Colonel

English of the Chemical Warfare Service asking for a song. Hot diggity! I met with Captain Art Parks to get some of the corps's background for the lyrics and he said, "First of all, mustard gas tears out the lining of the throat."

"Good material for a song," I said. And then he went on about smoke screens and garbage disposal, which dampened my enthusiasm still further, but only momentarily. I asked him what's the command when a chemical detail is supposed to start disposal operation and he said, "Fire up!" and I said, "That's it, Captain," and that night I finished it: "Fire Up—Carry on to Victory!"

Everybody liked it fine, and in the next issue of *Variety* there was a box on the front page headed CHEMICAL WARFARE SERVICE HAS NEW OFFICIAL SONG. Now this was more like it, and I went on to read the article. "The Chemical Warfare Service has just officially adopted a new song for the corps. It is by one of the corps's own enlisted men and is titled 'Gas-House Gus.' " Now I admit discouragement began to creep in.

Just then the doorbell rang and there was Sandy Cummings, who used to work on the old *Good News* show, only now he was a captain in the cavalry with boots you could see your face in, and spurs, and jeepers, it gave you the old whips and jingles just to look on him and you know, before he got out of there, I had written "Hit the Leather" for the cavalry.

Captain Cummings took it back to Fort Riley with him and I got a wonderful letter from his commanding officer and a phonograph record from the whole gang, and two weeks later the good old horse cavalry, as such, was mechanized and that was that.

Now I was getting discouraged and thought I'd take a run down to San Diego to see off a buddy of mine, Bernie Milligan, who had joined the Marine Corps and was shoving off for overseas, and this is as good a time as any to remark that he was the first marine to land in Tokyo.

Anyway, Bernie and I ended up that night in a San Diego burleyque, and as we walked down the aisle the curtain went up, and down the runway came six queens, grinding and bumping, singing "Gangway, You Rats, Gangwaaaaaaay" (Bump)!

The next day I was walking down Vine Street and I met a friend of mine about my own age with a proud look on his kisser. "What's with you?" I said, and he said, "Guess what! I just joined up. Why don't you?"

And twenty-four hours later I was in the Army.

31. LIKE EVERYBODY ELSE, I DIDN'T LOOK forward to the scientific assembly-line life in uniform. Of course when the government shopped for the Army, they had to buy ten million of everything, so it was "scientific assembly line" or else.

But even in normal times it seems we Americans just naturally accept scientific assembly-line improvements anyway—hell or high water—because we're so afraid of being the fellow on the bank of the Hudson River yelling, "It won't amount to nuthin'," at Robert Fulton. Or being the farmer looking at his first airplane wheeling over the south forty, shaking his head and saying, " 'Tain't so." Or of being Columbus and Galileo doubters—or Socrates scoffers.

We remember only too well that when the man spilled something on the stove that turned out to be rubber, or ruminated on the teakettle's whistle, or hooked the door key onto the tail of a kite, or parlayed you-know-what up to 606, all the people hollered, "It won't amount to nuthin'," or " 'Tain't so."

So I say hooray for Lum and Abner who courageously stuck to that big sure-enough pipe organ in Studio G at NBC for their broadcasts, which really sounded like something musical instead of the "educated static" we gotta listen to on so many programs since somebody invented the electric organ.

Could it be that because we're afraid of being progress impeders we may have lost our discrimination and are possibly being pushed around by "scientific achievement"?

Hooray for penicillin. Hooray for sulpha. But I have to come right out and claim that a real hunk of honest ice beats those little artificial melt-while-you-look-at-'em ice cubes forty ways from breakfast. And if you think that that fancy factory-packed box of ice cream can compare with the hand-packed oyster-pails-with-the-little-wire-handles kind, then your taster is on the blink. Right here in this town over at Wil Wright's, they've thrown out all the fancy ice-cream-making machinery, and a man sits there all night with a canoe paddle, so help me, and makes the ice cream entirely by hand, by paddle.

And what in the world is happening to cheese? Just think of a good honest hunk of rat cheese—

the kind they invented cheesecloth for—or a real brick of Wisconsin with those fine bubbly holes, or a creamy, rubbery slab of Monterey jack, and take your choice among any of those and any one of the triple-refined, silver-papered, sissified, two-by-four packages of creamed this or molded that.

Now I don't want to get in wrong with the retail merchants or the Better Business Bureau or the Board of Education. All I'm saying is, we get pushed around every once in a while by science, and if you'd rather have beer from a can than a barrel, and ice cream in a lousy little stale cup than a big fat waffle cone, drown me out—that's all—shout me down.

Well, anyhow, back to the Army, and who do you suppose should be the first guy transferred to my outfit? Abe Damon-and-Pythias Meyer—and was he a sad sack in his corporal's uniform!

We were in what was called the Armed Forces Radio Service, the production center for all overseas radio programs, and somebody ought to write a story of AFRS someday—musicians, actors, and writers getting up in the morning to fool around with M-1's and infiltration.

Sid Silvers used to be "the man in the box" in Phil Baker's vaudeville act. I think he was also Bottle on Mr. Baker's radio show some years ago. Anyway, he was in the Army and was assigned to us at AFRS, and on his very first day he was told to report to the Music Department at Twentieth Century-Fox tomorrow morning at eight-thirty to handle a *Command Performance* detail. "*Command Performance!*" Sid thought. "Been in this outfit only one day and right away they put me on *Command Performance*, their crack show!"

They gave him an Army truck to drive out to the studio in, and all the way out he was thinking up his pet routines and wondering whether he would be acting with Jack Benny or Red Skelton or who. At the gate the policeman directed him to the Music Department and he walked in the door into a whole set of drums, xylophones, timpani, and cathedral chimes.

"You from AFRS?" the boy in the office said.

"Yeah," said Sid. "The other actors here yet?"

"What actors?" said the kid. "The Army wanted to borrow these instruments for tonight's show. Take it easy with those cymbals and be sure and have that stuff back here by eight in the morning."

I told this story to the orchestra the next day at rehearsal and the bass player, Private Jud De Naut, laughed so hard he dropped his bass and split it wide open. It took about two weeks to get it fixed, and meantime the post had to rent one for him to use. When Jud found out this bass was costing the Army seven dollars a day rental, he looked off into space with a pathetic sort of wistful expression and said, "They get *me* for a dollar sixty-five."

The day he joined our outfit we had a pretty hot schedule, having had seven or eight complete shows on the fire, starting with *Melody Round-up* at 8 A.M., followed by *At Ease*, *Intermezzo*, *Jubilee*, two *Personal Albums*, and wound up with *Command Performance* and *Mail Call* at twelve-thirty that night. Private De Naut could just make it out the door, dragging his bass behind him. He passed the adjutant, who was standing in the parking lot, and barely managing a broken-down salute, said, "Sir, where do I go to surrender?"

I guess the greatest radio program of all time was the Dick Tracy hour-and-a-half *Command Performance* dreamed up and produced by Sergeant Bob Welch with the following cast:

> *Bing Crosby as Dick Tracy*
> *Dinah Shore as Tess Trueheart*
> *Judy Garland as Snowflake*
> *Bob Hope as Flat-top*
> *Frank Morgan as Vitamin Flintheart*
> *Jerry Colonna as Chief of Police*
> *The Andrews Sisters as the Summer Sisters*
> *Jimmy Durante as the Mole*
> *Frank Sinatra as Shaky, and*
> *Cass Daley as Gravel Gertie*

That was not the first time the Voice and the Groaner were on a radio show together, by the way. However, we did present their first meeting. It was some months earlier, also on *Command Performance*. I'll never forget that one either.

We were one *Command* show behind, so we had to record a double-header that day to keep on schedule. The first one was the now historic first appearance of Mr. Crosby and Mr. Sinatra together on the same show, and we had Bob Hope in there for good measure. A man named Glenn Wheaton was the originator of *Command Performance* and he wrote this Crosby-Sinatra duel and it was a honey. Well, anyway, we finished that one and cleared out the audience, then loaded the theater up again and started the second show, which was to be an all-girl affair except for Ken Carpenter, the permanent announcer through the whole war.

According to plan, Connie Haines opened the show and Sinatra, Crosby, and Hope came bursting out on the stage demanding seats. We had a small love seat on the stage with a mike in front of it, and those three were squeezed onto that small couch, Sinatra in the middle, and of course there have never been such ad libs in the history of the radio business.

Now just for variety and to show you the audaciousness of Glenn Wheaton's programing, the all-girl cast included not only every top femme singing star you ever heard of, but also Lotte

Lehmann, one of the great lieder singers of our time.

Now Madame Lehmann isn't what you'd call a slip of a girl exactly, and she was swathed in gardenias, and with a big feather hat in front and quite a train in back she made a real interesting entrance.

Bob Hope took a look as she came sailing in and whispered across Sinatra's lap to Crosby, "Hey, Cros, I don't think she's going to be able to take off!"

Well, Crosby is an old trouper and managed to keep a straight face, though his larynx was jumping around completely out of control. Even Hope himself had to hang onto the ropes and stare at the cracks in the floor, fighting to keep from breaking up—while Crosby concentrated feverishly on counting the pages in his script. But Sinatra lost control altogether and was red in the face and was gasping and struggling for breath.

Now considering all the ad libs that had been going on, the GI audience there in the studio, who didn't know Lotte Lehmann from Cab Calloway, were hotter than a firecracker, and this audience had been screaming with hysterical laughter ever since the show started, and they were charged with dynamite by this time, and the slightest movement of Bob Hope's eyebrow would have set them off, and they were sure this lady was part of a routine anyway, and any minute now they expected her to raise her skirts and roller-skate off with striped stockings.

Madame Lehmann was to sing Brahms's "Lullaby," and as she wasn't used to singing it in English, she had the words written down on a piece of paper.

Well, she started to sing, and I got to thinking how horrible it would be if the guys out front would lose control and get to laughing. Not knowing what else to do, I turned around while conducting and glared at the audience, trying to convey the idea that this was on the level, but as I turned back to my music stand Madame Lehmann raised—heaven help us—a lorgnette to peer at the words with, and I said to myself, Good night, all.

But by this time the guys were really listening, and as Madame Lehmann soared into the second stanza they knew they were hearing something great, and that wonderful singer ended up with the entire audience eating out of her hand. She left the stage bowing and smiling in an uproar of applause and whistling and stamping, completely unaware of the fact that she had just sailed through a situation that could have been the most awful moment in musical history.

32. BACK IN 1879 "VANITY FAIR" PUB-
lished a picture of Verdi, maybe the greatest opera
composer of all time. Under the picture some non-
immortal caption writer brushed this genius off
with the following remark: "Giuseppe Verdi,
composer. His music is the music of the times,
tuneful—pleasant—and shallow."

I guess it's human nature to enjoy seeing critics
occasionally fall on their faces like that.

I went to a dinner party for a critic one time.
No, not Olin Downes. I positively don't hold
grudges. Anyhow, I got there early and the hostess's home had been done over and she was showing this critic through it. I joined the tour and
she showed us the library, then the den and the
music room, and finally she said, "And now I want
you to see the head!"

Well, I nearly swallowed my teeth and immediately thought, My, my, my, the war certainly has
left its mark on social small talk, and just as I

opened my mouth to make some ribald remark to put the hostess at her ease and show her I could go along with a gag, the critic beat me to it with a lusty comment he must have picked up in the men's room between the acts at Minsky's—wherewith the poor shaken lady led us down into her sunken living room and pointed to a brand-new bust of an elder member of her family and, by golly, it was a head.

It's one thing to be contemptuous of small talk, but it's another thing to be able to do something about it.

I have finally gotten to the point of figuring out a way to avoid small talk in people's vestibules—all that "good night" fumbling, like, "Well, I tell you—ah—er—ah—see you during the week—you know—around? Thanks again—ahhh—swell evening and—er—thanks again—a million—ah—ah——"

And the answer isn't to put such broken-down phrases into dialect either, like: "Okey, keed, ol' keed, ol' boy, ol' socks—had a ska-rump-shus evenin'—you-all sho' nuff do set a mighty fancy table-a-vittles, you-all do—sho' nuff—sho' sho' sho'—and I must say I'm mighty fonda your ol' man's liquor—ha-ha—mighty fond—you bet—ha-ha."

I've found out you can dodge all that like this: (1) get up, (2) find the hostess, (3) say thank you and shake her hand, (4) GO.

But so far as the evening itself is concerned, I'm a miserable failure at escaping any kind of small talk. I tried once to pattern my social behavior after a friend of mine who used to wrap up ample portions of the peas or lima beans during dinner, and even some of the salad, in various spare handkerchiefs he had on him. He'd tuck the vegetables nicely into one of these handkerchiefs and put it back in his pocket with no change of expression or explanation. This either provoked gay conversation or none whatever, but definitely no small talk.

I never could pull it off myself, though. My last try at eccentricity was at a party in the Presidio in San Francisco, beautiful San Francisco! Things were pretty dull, so I took out the stud from the middle of my shirt and went from guest to guest. If they didn't mention it at all, I accused them playfully of not being frank, or of being cowardly, or different things. I did provoke a little gay conversation, it seems to me, until one of the guests —a Mrs. Mischa Elman—said, "I can only say you are very rude and impolite, also untidy and slightly revolting, going around with your underwear showing."

So now I am not eccentric any more and I just make small talk with everybody else, and if I get caught off balance I don't worry about it.

People nearly all react the same when they get

caught off balance. When a magician asks you up on the stage to help him with a trick, he catches you off balance, and no matter who you are, you walk up the steps, clumsy-like and feeling unpressed and awkward, and of course the magician knows this, so he also knows that in your condition he could tie any number of "fake" knots right in front of your eyes and you'd never know the difference.

At a Hollywood party one night a little two-by-four magician was hired for a few bucks to entertain the guests. Standing right there in the living room, he asked Bob Montgomery and Walter Pidgeon to help him with a trick, and those two internationally celebrated gentlemen got up, all feet and ears, and grinned foolishly even as you and I, while the ten-buck-an-evening prestidigitator oozed glamour and sleek charm in his immaculately gleaming rented tuxedo.

Ever see Gene Krupa step out from behind his drums? The very moment he does, that million-dollar smile seems to fade into a common ordinary garden-variety grin.

Here's something else you won't believe. I got to thinking once about all the ulcers and high blood pressures that show business in Hollywood seems to aid and abet, and I said to myself, Maybe it's pretty ridiculous to always go at lunch time right from the office or studio into a mad frenzy of guys in a restaurant, talking nothing but show business, because that way you never really give your poor digestive system half a chance at that number-one sandwich and coffee which you daily throw into your complicated eating machinery, going a mile a minute on the dead run, as you might say.

So in a burst of Alexander Botts enthusiasm, I started the No-Business Lunch as a glorious and magnificent effort toward preserving both the esophagus and the art of conversation. Well, I made great plans and invited a lot of important people from different walks of life: Rupert Hughes, novelist; Sid Strotz, NBC vice-president; Bill Goodwin, actor; Frank Loesser, poet, song writer, and producer; Dr. Suess, artist, author, and cartoonist; Chet Lauck, of Lum and Abner; Norman Tyre, barrister and proctor; and John Gillen, radio-station owner and industrialist. And between the longest, deadliest lulls you ever heard, the conversation consisted entirely of speculation about whether it would rain in the Rose Bowl the following week, and if so, how this circumstance would affect the outcome of the football game, and the only reason the lunch lasted two hours was because nobody could think of an exit line, and why do I get into these things?

That's what usually happens when you get caught off balance, just like Groucho Marx walking into a roomful of strangers and somebody says, "Be funny, Groucho." It just can't be done.

33. SOME THINGS GET SO ESTABLISHED IN your make-up as luxuries that you never get to the point where you can lean back and enjoy them. With me it's Welch's grape juice. To this day I never seem to think I can afford those little ten-cent bottles.

All that stuff in the bon-voyage and Christmas baskets had me buffaloed, too, for a good many years—those small jars of crab legs and trout pâté and minced chestnuts and olives stuffed with anchovies, and brandied this, that, and the other. Whenever I'd get one of those baskets I'd always set those bottles and cans and jars way back on the shelf to wait for a special occasion. You just naturally didn't open those things up and eat 'em right there in the kitchen, like.

Well, one day I met a man with a fantastic curiosity about those jars and things, and he sold me on the idea that those fancy vittles can get like a bride's wedding ring—if she doesn't take it off the very first day, the idea of taking it off at all gives her the heebie-jeebies, and her whole life gradually becomes second fiddle to that little gold band—just like those small jars and cans back on the shelf actually get to high-hatting you, and the first thing you know, you can never bring yourself to open any of 'em up at all.

So the next time somebody sent me one of those baskets, I tore off the ribbon, grabbed a can opener, took a deep breath, and charged in, and do you know, a lotta that stuff tastes just wonderful?

That man with the fantastic curiosity has a name, and it is Harold Lloyd, and if you live in Beverly Hills, sooner or later you meet Harold Lloyd because he's just as civic-minded in Beverly, you might say, as Carl Parker is in Mason City—Better Business Bureau, Chamber of Commerce, and, for all I know, teaches the men's Sunday-school class in the lecture room just before morning service.

Well, anyway, shortly after I joined the Army, Mr. Lloyd and I were visiting, not only about how to put those Christmas baskets in their place but also about this new phenomenon that had just descended on an unsuspecting America by the name of Sinatra. Mr. Lloyd has two daughters who were bobby-socks age then, and was he confused.

"What does this Sinatra have, anyway?" he said. "Such swooning and groaning goes on over at our house every time anybody mentions his name, which is all the time, because those girls can change any subject—whether it's how to pronounce Armageddon, or the fantail belt on a rotary snowplow—right back to Sinatra."

"You got me," I said, not knowing Frankie then as well as I do now, "but if you'd like to see for yourself, he's on *Command Performance* tomorrow night. Bring the girls."

"If I didn't, I might as well leave home," said Mr. Lloyd.

After the show the next night the Lloyds came backstage. Harold only wears glasses in his pictures (and only rims at that), so people seldom recognize him.

I introduced the girls to Frankie, and whereas Mrs. Lloyd managed a fairly adequate acknowledgment, the girls just driveled and druveled and gurgled and googled like Ethel Merman reacting to Ray Middleton in *Annie Get Your Gun*, only more so. But when Frankie found out it was Harold Lloyd, it was his turn to google and goggle. He finally came up with, "Gee, Mr. Lloyd, it's sure an honor to meet you."

Well, you know the old wheeze about a prophet in his own front yard. All the way home Peggy and Gloria Lloyd hysterically gasped to each other over and over again: "*IMAGINE*, FRANKIE SAID HE WAS HONORED TO MEET *DAD!*"

Harold Lloyd is a fine gentleman, good amateur magician, great actor, and one of the "good guys." He has a nine-hole golf course in his back yard and an orange grove and a grape arbor in his front yard.

A grape arbor in his front yard.

Say, whatever happened to grape baskets? And it's funny, now I think of it, that Iowa isn't exactly famous as grape country at all, really, and yet we kids were brought up on Concord grapes, which, if you don't know it, you never chew but kind of squeeze them into your throat and swaller 'em whole. Every once in a while you'd peel the blue skin away and just eat the purple velvet layer, which was the good part, although now it hardly sounds worth the effort.

But we could never have gotten along without grape baskets. There was one for a catchall just inside the cellar door that had the ball of string in it and the tacks and a few shingle nails—also a couple orange-colored rubber bands off preserve jars, the small screw driver, and some spools. The spools made good pulleys to rig up the "telegraph" from our attic window over to my cousin Phil's.

There was usually a dead light globe in the grape basket too. We used to try to use it for a sun glass to burn holes in things with. Doesn't

217

seem that it worked—not like Grampa's magnifying glass at least.

Before closing the cellar door the big thing was to be sure to turn off the light. The switch made a funny little singing vibration as you turned it to where it said "off."

Mama used to line a grape basket with newspaper and fill it with lettuce, which we'd sell once a week for fifteen cents a basket to the Vermilyea Restaurant. Another grape basket was on the attic stairs full of shells Aunt Bonnie brought from the ocean. Iowa kids didn't know much about oceans and mountains. We could play with these shells in the bathtub on Saturdays as a special inducement to bathe, and how we listened in the pink mouth of the big one to hear the waves roar.

Kind things were: those shells, Grampa's vise on the workbench in the old house where we made swords out of laths and changed garbage-can covers into glittering shields, Miss Ida Stilson's laugh, and the vacuumy stillness of Mr. Bird's thread store which soaked up the gentle bleeps of the canary over in the corner. Mr. Bird looked like a canary and gave us thread boxes to make May baskets out of. It sounded nice the way Mr. Jackson called Papa by his first name, "Good morning, John." Mr. Jackson and Papa registered the voters each election in Macauley's garage. And more kind things were my cousin Jeannie's voice and that soft spatula she used to take the butterscotch out of the pie tin with after it cooled, and Mr. Robert's beard and blue suit and G.A.R. button on Decoration Day, and Jim Griffith's dimples through the barbershop window, and the handkerchief in Papa's overcoat pocket, always warm and smelling of Juicy Fruit and Prince Albert, and "Aunt" Marie's "Anybody home?" She was the lady with the Swedish accent three houses down the block, and she was also Mama's best friend. She used to say "forth and back" instead of "back and forth," and I'm beginning to realize she was right. Pick up a trombone. I'd sure like to see you move the slide any place but forth.

Mrs. Brice brought post cards back from Hawaii burned at the edges from a real volcano, and a little lantern made out of a round, prickly balloon fish, also some lava. We took them to show off at school. And Uncle Olin, visiting from Orange City, always brought a green or red lantern full of candy he bought for us on the train.

You could almost measure your growing up by candy. The jawbreakers that used to change color in your mouth. You'd spend a whole day on them just to get at that thing in the middle—what was that?—a seed or something like it. And all the greenish-black varieties of licorice. Then came jelly beans, gumdrops, and Necco wafers, all different colors, though we suspected there were more white ones; then you graduated to Necco wafers, all chocolate! And then the white taffy at the Olympia Candy Kitchen that Mr. Manusus used to break up with a little silver hammer, and finally the chocolate creams wrapped in gold paper with a pair of little silver tongs in every box.

Unkind things were: big kids playing leapfrog with little kids, the big ones landing full tilt on those small backs from five feet away. Also check-reins. Mama used to run out in the street and grab a horse with a high checkrein and hang on, while one of us kids ran for Mr. Nutting with his Humane Society badge.

34. EVERYBODY HAS HIS OWN MEMORIES of V-J Day. We were in the middle of recording *Command Performance* and I couldn't begin to put the events or my feelings down on paper any more than you could yours, though they are as clear and distinct as though it all happened yesterday.

I was already on terminal leave and was itching to put on a colored necktie, loud socks, and suspenders. Anyhow, it was all over and I started to think about getting back on the air again.

One day as I was walking through the NBC parking lot, a fine-looking GI with that happy ruptured duck sewed on his uniform handed me a letter. He was about twenty-five and had a lot more stuff hanging on his chest besides that golden chariot wheel. The letter was a typical mother's letter: "Take care of my boy, please. Help him to meet good people." You know—all those things a mother would write.

Sure—my kindly teacher, the elegant, witty, fastidious, flute-playing genius, Georges Barrère, was gone, and the letter was from Mrs. Georges Barrère, and the blond veteran was their little son Jean all grown up.

The first day I put on civilian clothes I went over to the Hollywood Brown Derby and, looking for a job and all, I half expected a man to come up with a wild look in his eye and say, "You playa da floot? Good! Standa youself under da clock," but instead Chet Lauck of *Lum and Abner* stopped by my table to say hello. We fell to talking about old vaudeville acts and Chet said his favorite headliner was a fellow who used to open seriously in a cutaway and end with a breakaway piano, throwing stuff all over the stage. "Let's see, what was his name again? Got it right on the tip of my tongue."

Well, we thought and we thought. Ray Noble was sitting across the aisle and I called over a description of this vaudevillian and he said, "Got his name right on the tip of my tongue—starts with an R." He turned to the people sitting behind him and asked them. They said, "Sure, we know who you mean. Got his name right on the tip of our tongue—starts with an L."

Now this went on from table to table, and in eight minutes it looked as though the whole restaurant, including Bob Cobb, the owner, was playing "still water," everybody sitting stock-still, staring off into space, not touching their food or anything.

Suddenly it hit me—"Al Trahan!" Ray Noble heard me and passed it along, nodding and smiling, and everybody passed it along to everybody else and immediately the usual hubbub started buzzing over the booths again and the tableau had come back to life.

After Chet left my table, Lou Sidney stopped by and said, "Hey, Meredith, we'd like you to be musical director of M.G.M.," and presently Sid Strotz came over and said, "Want to move back home to Sunset and Vine and take over the music for Hollywood NBC?"

I guess that any way you'd mention those offers it would sound like bragging, but it seems to me it's human nature to brag on yourself, and if you don't, it's maybe not so much that you aren't itching to but more because you're afraid people will say, "Look at him brag."

However that may be, I don't know of a more grateful feeling than to come out of a three-year hitch and run into that kind of flattery, because even though I fought the entire war without leaving Hollywood, that Army suit takes you into a whole new world—mentally, physically, and financially— and my ribbonless chest was full of apprehension at stumbling back into civilian life again. Also, being so used in the Army to building radio programs that had a make-you-the-better-for-having-heard-it ingredient, wouldn't I miss just doing straight entertainment shows again that were only funny or absorbing or tuneful?

And another thing—having had a chance in the Army to rare back and take a good look at radio, it seemed to me that a certain amount of radio time was being wasted on some pretty dull stuff, particularly on musical programs, like, "We bring to you now a special arrangement of a beautiful melody, designed to whisk you away for a wisp of a while from the cares of the workaday world," or still worse, the comedy exchange between the singer and the announcer: "What are you going to sing next, Joe?" and the singer says, " 'After You've Gone,' " and the announcer says, "Gee, I wish you'd sing now so I can hear it," and the singer says, "No, no, you don't understand—the name of the song is 'After You've Gone,' " and the announcer says, "Oh," and then the singer sings "After You've Gone."

And how about the dignified but ultra-poetic approach where the announcer says in hushed tones, "As the last rays of the dying sun fade away and the moon mounts into the sky, there comes that magic twilight hour which marks the meeting of—[Pause]—night and day." And the orchestra then plays "Night and Day."

I can't get a load of stuff like that without feeling like old Martha Rinsenhauser, Mama's first "hard girl," who ate some green peaches one summer and then contributed to our family memoirs by delivering herself of this magnificent phrase, "Oh, Meesus Villson—if I could only puke." One little gem in particular affects me that way: "And now the orchestra asks the musical question— 'Who?'"

The sponsor pays good money for the time on the air and isn't it kind of ridiculous to use any part of it on horrible, crumby garbage verbiage like that? I said to myself.

Then the commercials. Criminy—there must be some way of telling about the product in some interesting way that wouldn't conjure up Martha Rinsenhauser every fifteen minutes.

After kicking all that around for a few weeks I thought I'd toy with a musical show of my own and I ended up with a thirty-eight piece orchestra featuring Ethel Smith's electric organ, Les Paul's electric guitar, and Burl Ives's electrifying folk-song singing, plus no talk or announcements at all, but instead a lot of sponsor-identification tricks, including the use of the Sono-Vox and a male chorus that chanted the commercial in unison.

The Sono-Vox, by the way, is the device they use for the talking train that goes "Bromo-Seltzer, Bromo-Seltzer, Bromo-Seltzer." The operator (usually a charming girl named Janet Eberhart) holds two disks against her throat, and the sound (a train, a foghorn, or any other sound) is actually fed electrically through her neck into her mouth. She forms the words "Bromo-Seltzer" or "Beeeeeeee—ooooooo," or whatever else you want her to say, around that sound with her tongue, teeth, and lips—just the way she would if she were talking, except she uses the artificial electric sounds being currented into her throat instead of her own vocal chords. Isn't that interesting?

Anyhow, my program was a big success except for one small detail—nobody bought it. This was because it cost fifteen thousand dollars a week, and that was supposed to be too expensive for a musical show.

A fellow named Hooper runs a company that hires people to phone you and say, "What program are you listening to, if you please?" and from that and other information they compile the fortnightly Hooper Report which tells you how many people are listening to your show. One Hooper point is equal to a million people in round numbers, so if you have a Hooper rating of twenty-five to thirty, like the Bob Hope show, you have an audience of twenty-five to thirty million listeners and you are very happy, and if you have a Hooper rating of 1.3, like "How to get more out of your factory," you go out and shoot yourself.

What I wanted to say was that up till then no musical show had ever gotten beyond a rating of ten or so with the exception of the old *Fitch Band Wagon*, which doesn't count because it was sandwiched in between Jack Benny and Edgar Bergen, both with very fat twenty-six-average Hoopers, and you could read the Brooklyn telephone directory in that Fitch spot and get pretty close to a twenty rating on account of it was more bother to tune out than just to let 'er ride, and besides, you didn't want to run the risk of missing Bergen.

The *Hit Parade* rating is high for a musical, but that's because a lot of people like to know what the country's top tunes are, and *Manhattan Merry-Go-Round* does pretty good, too, but (1) it's been on for a few thousand weeks, and (2) it's fascinating to hear the tremolo in that man's voice when he says, "Doctor Lyonnnnnnns' tooth powder."

At any rate, it seems to be generally good practice in the radio business to pay not more than one thousand dollars per Hooper point for a program—so if the show cost fifteen thousand dollars, you'd have to expect a Hooper rating of fifteen, which everybody said couldn't be done with a musical, so I went to bed with my fine electrical show, a sadder but to some extent wiser man, for I immediately began to figure out a musical show that wouldn't cost fifteen thousand dollars.

I forgot to say that I didn't go to M.G.M. as musical director, or to NBC either, because of the desire to be my own boss, as you might say, and dream up my own radio program, but just about this time George Burns and Gracie Allen had been bought by Maxwell House Coffee and George wanted me to join his cast, and there I was happily back with Maxwell House and still playing a bucolic stooge along with the music.

35. EVERY PROFESSION HAS ITS TERMI-
nology and its lingo. I first discovered this in New
York when I used to ride on the Tremont Avenue
cross-town streetcar to play in Sol Klein's Crescent
Theatre orchestra.

My hours were so regular that I used to get the
same conductor most of the time. One night my
conductor friend was sad and one night glad, de-
pending, so I learned, on the equipment of the
car. "Will I be glad to get to the barn tonight!
Had the stiffest clock and the roughest door of
the whole Third Avenue system." This meant that
every time he had to ring up a fare it was twice as
hard because the "clock" he had to ring the fare
up on worked harder than it should, and also every
time anybody got on or off it was harder to open
the door on account of the bottom of this door
rubbed the floor of the car.

This experience made me feel "in the know"
about the streetcar business, and I've somehow re-

membered it, for let me see—nearly a quarter of a century.

I guess now that I think of it we must have a lot of professional lingo in the radio business that we take for granted like the trolley conductor does the stiff clock and the rough door. For example, there is the hitch-hike and the cow-catcher. These are the inside, "backstage" names for the extra little commercials about companion products that are sandwiched in just at the beginning and before the end of radio shows.

Now the reason why radio programs became cursed with hitch-hikes and cow-catchers is simply because the local stations got the habit of selling local announcements between each program. This practice meant that for twenty-five dollars or so you could hook onto a crack thirty-thousand-dollar network show with some tinkling little jingle about the advantages of your pawnshop or bird-seed store or whatever. So instead of getting the networks to do something about scraping off these twenty-five-dollar barnacles, the big sponsors tried to correct the evil by protecting the beginning and end of their own shows with still more products —so nowadays you get something like this every half-hour:

> (Closing Commercial): Next week the makers of "Joy" soup will again bring you the "Joy" program—hmm mm good!"

(*Then the hitch-hike!*)

(Bell) (Announcer): What is that ring-ing sound I hear?

(Girls' Trio): It's time for all you sluggish boobs To drink your "Happy Bouillon Cubes."

(Sound effects): Slurp—Slurp—Slurp.

(Back to "Joy" M.C.): And so once again good night from the makers of "Joy" soup— hmm mm good.

(Orchestra plays theme till faded)

(Now comes the local spot)

(Local Announcer): Crunch Crunch Crunch Crunch—will you wed me, honey-bunch?

(Girl): I'll love and cherish you forever more If you'll buy my ring at Crunch's High-grade Jewelry Store.

(Then the time signal)

(Gong) (Transcription)

(Announcer): Pullova watch time—ten seconds before eight o'clock. Give him a Pullova—IT TICKS!!

(The next program leads off with a cow-catcher.)

Drink Kucumber Krush for that pale green look!

(And then the orchestra plays the theme and fades for the announcer): Once again

—Squirts Jerkhins bring you *"THE PICKLE HOUR."*

So, all in all, you've had six commercials about six different products in the space of fifty-five seconds.

The last hitch-hike we had was built around a bird whistle and a three-note tune. The hitch-hike entourage moved in on us for rehearsals and auditions to select the whistle, the proper quality of voices for the three notes, and also the proper orchestra accompaniment. All in all, the group included a producer, an assistant producer, a music arranger, a whistler, three singers, and a copy writer, and if you think I'm kidding look in on any network studio any day or night on the hour and the half-hour.

Radio is show business, though. Can't deny it at all, even though there are some basic differences between it and the traditional theater that loom up like a prop fireplace. For instance, any kind of performer I ever knew, including the guy with the trained seal and the Shakespearean actor with the frayed cuffs, was always on fire with an unquenchable superiority. Boy, did he wow 'em in Peoria—did he kill 'em in Oshkosh. "We took fourteen bows, see, and everybody's saying we'll be moved into next-to-closing by Saturday." Nobody had to tell *him* he was good.

But in the radio business the world's greatest performers are rapidly turning into a curious kind of pathetic starveling, hungry for a crumb of any kind of compliment, and parched for the ripple of a little honest, unprodded applause. Just stand outside the artists' entrance at NBC. A household word with a million dollars comes out after his broadcast, and the kid in the parking lot says to him, "Hiya, sweetheart, heard the tail end of your show tonight. Not bad." The star's grateful expression is pitiful: "You *did* hear it *really*? Was it all right? Did you notice the sound-effect man step on my laugh with that lousy door slam?"

"Wasn't bad."

"Really? How'd you like the new voice Elliot used for the cabdriver?"

"Okay, okay."

"Sounded good, didn't you think?"

"Not bad at all."

"And how about when Elvia broke up? Huh? No, no, that was on the level. She said 'Good-by' *after* the door slam, and of course the audience screamed bloody murder. Did you ever hear such a yak in your life?"

"Loud, all right."

"Well, Elvia just broke up, that's all. Couldn't read another line. Every time she'd open her mouth she'd go up again."

"I figured it was a phony bust-up for laughs."

"No, no, kid—honest. I'm telling you she was on the level. *Really* broke up higher'n a kite."

"Well, show wasn't bad."

"Sure glad to hear you say that. Thanks, thanks a lot! Gee—thanks—so long!" And he floats off to one of his Cadillac convertibles on a river of grateful tears.

36. MAXWELL HOUSE HAS BEEN ON Thursday for years and years since way back before *Captain Henry's Show Boat.*

Funny how Thursdays have always had a special kind of flavor for me, starting with my *Saturday Evening Post* route in Mason City. When I was a kid, the *Post* came out on Thursdays—nowadays it comes out on Tuesdays. Maybe in the next generation it will be pushed back to Saturday again—wouldn't that be interesting? Anyhow, I bought this *Post* route for fifteen dollars from Merlin Bushgens, and it included sixty customers —mostly doctors, dentists, and lawyers—with a few *Country Gentleman* and *Ladies' Home Journals* thrown in, also some good will on account of Merlin had a pleasant freckle-faced personality. Thursday, consequently, tasted different from any other day, on account of I delivered the *Posts* before school and collected after school and sold a few on Main Street (now Federal Avenue) before

235

supper. I used to ham up my sales talk plenty in front of the Idle Hour Theatre where Elsie Johanson sold tickets after school. She was my first real crush and I left most of the profits from my *Post* route at her ticket window, in the form of all-day suckers, little pink hearts with mottoes on them, or molasses-and-peanut-butter kisses from the ten-cent store.

I got up the nerve to ask her to a dance in the Knights of Pythias Hall one time—and I felt pretty good about my first attempt at the one-step, which consisted, as I think back, of a clumsy sort of march straight down the border of the dance floor to the corner and then a convulsive swing around to the left and continuing like that all the way around, with a triumphant look-Ma-I'm-dancing expression on my kisser.

I seemed to have something on the ball, though, because it was the first dance of the evening and the wax was fresh and everybody was slipping and sliding around but me. My success, however, as I soon discovered to my gulping horror, was only due to the mud-stained overshoes which I had forgotten to take off.

Thursdays, on the way home from selling *Posts*, I used to pass the Congregational Church, and there was a pretty good chance I'd meet Mr. Patchen, my piano teacher, who always ran over the organ music late Thursday afternoon for choir practice that night. So I invariably managed to be whistling "The Anvil Chorus" or the "Quartette" from *Rigoletto* when I passed within earshot of the church, to kind of impress Mr. Patchen with my good musical taste.

The "different" flavor of Thursday followed me into the New York Philharmonic's Thursday concerts in Carnegie Hall, and then Maxwell House, and even in the Army we did *Command Performance* every Thursday, so what with one thing or another, I've eaten my Thanksgiving turkey most of my life on the run, between concerts or rehearsals or delivering *Posts* or something.

Well, anyway, it's Thursday and it's 10:30 A.M., time for the Maxwell House dress rehearsal. We usually read the show through only twice, being as how we've already rehearsed on Wednesday. The writers and producers make slight suggestions about different inflections or the sound effects, and the engineer who controls the mikes marks his script according to what mike should be open at what time.

The orchestra arrives at one-thirty and we then rehearse the musical number, the musical commercial, and each bridge—usually twelve or fifteen seconds of music indicating the mood or scene changes or passing of time. By now it's probably four-thirty and the whole cast is reassembled for a once-over-lightly reading. At this session there

237

is a curious combination of it's-all-set-now relaxation and this-is-it tension, and everybody wants everybody else to do good, and show business and esprit and camaraderie begin to take over. George says, "Can we move?" Never "Let's start," or "Shall we begin"—always "Can we move?" And at five we're through reading and from five to five-fifteen we get nervous and at five-fifteen Bill Goodwin walks out onto the stage and starts the "warm-up."

This warm-up is a pre-show routine that is part of every radio program, and the idea is to get the audience in a gay receptive mood so they will feel like laughing and applauding. Seems a little silly, also strange, that we should do this in the radio business when it's not done in any other branch of entertainment. Wouldn't it be ridiculous for a fellow in the theater to come out before a stage show and say, "Now, ladies and gentlemen, we want you to relax and enjoy yourself. If you feel like laughing, by all means *GIVE*, and when you applaud make it *GOOD*, and now before introducing our stars I've got a little story here you may not have heard . . ." which is about the way a radio warm-up begins.

I guess the reason we do that in radio is because our shows are only a half-hour long and the audience has to be artificially stimulated and coaxed into a quick enthusiasm, so that the people are

238

ready to react immediately the program goes on the air.

On Fibber and Molly's show they invented the belly-laugh-just-as-you-hit-the-air type of warm-up. All the members of the cast are introduced as on the others shows, and then Fibber goes into his own particular version of telling the audience to relax, laugh loud, lean up to the mikes when they applaud, and so on, but all the time he keeps checking with the big oversize expensive-looking stop watch he has in his hand.

Finally, at exactly one second before air time by the big red hand on the studio clock, he throws the cue at Harlow Wilcox, the announcer, and then as though he had no further need for his magnificent watch, he casually tosses it over his shoulder. It hits the stage with a crash, and glass and springs and stuff fly all over, so at that precise one fifth of a second the audience screams with hysterical surprise and laughter and the engineer throws the switch and that's the way they go on the air every Tuesday night, with a big all-out holler.

Al Jolson always walks right down to the front and sits on the edge of the stage, jumps right up again, holding his pants, as if he has burned his sitter on the footlights, yelling "Cheez!" and the audience hollers like they were just let in on some unintentional piece of impromptu business.

This is one of the big tricks of radio, and the audience seems to fall for it every time—I mean pretending that cut-and-dried routines are accidental—like if Bill Goodwin insults George during the program, it's always sure-fire for George to walk over and peer into Bill's script as though something had been slipped in there that he hadn't known about. Everybody in the business resorts to that one when the laughs aren't coming strong enough.

Another favorite is the phony bust-up. If you deliver a comedy line that doesn't get anything, you puff out your face and hold your mouth and make like you can't read the next line from laughing so hard, and the audience will come through with a yak every time, even though they haven't any idea what they're laughing at—and they'll tell about it at home yet: "Well, sir, that fella who plays the doctor got laughing so hard, would you believe it, he couldn't go on with his script. Funny? I thought I'd die!"

Bob Hope either kisses his script after a big successful joke (which accounts for the unexplained double laugh you often hear on his show) or, if he's just laid an egg, he stabs at his script with his fingers like he's poking out its eyes— which guarantees a bigger laugh than if the lines had mopped up.

Jack Benny, of course, just turns to the audience

with that slow, tired, dead-pan look, which only insures every gag like it was underwritten by the Maharajah of Indore, the Bank of England, Wall Street, Fort Knox, and the U. S. Mint.

Anyhow, on George and Gracie's warm-up, Bill tells a joke and then introduces all of us and we come out and bow and sit on the stage, and then about three minutes before show time George and Gracie are introduced and they do a hunk of one of their old vaudeville sketches which sounds as funny and as fresh as it did in the old days, and as the second hand of the studio clock (plainly visible to the audience) sweeps closer and closer to air time, we all pretend to get nervouser and nervouser, and finally the red light under the clock goes on and we're off to the races, and we don't have to pretend to be nervous any more—we ARE.

37. WELL, AFTER FINISHING MY FIRST season back with Maxwell House since my Army discharge, there came the matter of a summer replacement, and George and Gracie wanted me to be it and I was anxious to get the job so I could try out my own musical. But I still hadn't figured out a way to do it that wouldn't be so danged expensive, so the sponsor and the agency finally decided that for economic reasons I had better go on with just a garden variety and-now-the-orchestra-asks-the-musical-question-who type of show and I got to thinking about Martha Rinsenhauser, and one day up at the agency office, discussing the plan of the summer program, I started sounding off: "Of course the program will be mostly music—WHY WOULDN'T IT BE? Americans are crazy about music, aren't they? They buy millions of phonograph records, don't they, and every kid knows who played second alto with Duke Ellington in 1930—but can't we make the program INTERESTING? Do we have to say, 'And now the conductor raises his musical baton and asks the musical question: "Who?" ' Even if we only say, 'Did you know there are more cats in New York City than there are people?' an unfamiliar fact like that will get the listeners' attention, maybe, and then I could say: 'I threw in that unfamiliar fact because our opening number is an unfamiliar number and I wanted to show you how interesting an unfamiliar thing can be and why should an unfamiliar number scare anybody? After all, "Stardust" was unfamiliar before Hoagy Carmichael wrote it, wasn't it?' And then we could play some nice refreshing tune instead of always 'Make Believe' from *Show Boat* to whisk you away for a wisp of a while from the cares of the workaday world!"

Well, the agency people at the meeting didn't know I was just shooting off my mouth—they thought I was ad libbing some pretty good material for the program, so before I knew it the script girl had taken down my spleen in shorthand and I went on the air that summer, June 6, 1946, to be exact, with my own show, and if you happened to be among those who heard it (we opened with a 4.5 Hooper) you heard the above remarks, seeing as that's exactly what I said on the opening program that night, starting with, "Of course the program will be mostly music. WHY WOULDN'T IT BE . . ."

Well, before we knew it, the summer was over and guess what our Hooper rating was? Yeah—4.5. But anyhow, maybe summer Hoopers don't mean anything on account of many million listeners can be catching your show in the car or at the beach where the Hooper people can't get 'em by phone. That's one nice thing about radio surveys—you can interpret them according to whether your rating is up or down—your belief in their accuracy is connected to your rating like a Siamese twin.

If your rating is up you say, "After all, the Hooper comes the closest to being a real accurate yardstick. It certainly is the best measuring device we've had, and I for one will accept it till we get something better." And if your rating is down: "After all, what does the Hooper mean, actually? You can't tell me there isn't something very screwy about the whole setup. If you ask me, I say it's the scourge of the radio business, creating entirely false values. Did you ever know anybody who ever knew anybody who had ever been called on the phone by any Hooper representative? Well, neither did I—and how about the rural areas and the small towns and the . . ." So on and so on and so on.

Well, anyway, thanks to Benton and Bowles and George Burns and General Foods, I'd had my fling and whadayaknow—before August set in Canada Dry bought the show for fall.

It all happened because one day the side door to the *Daily Variety* office on Vine Street got smashed. Newspaper offices being traditionally untidy, and California weather being traditionally tidy, not to say dependable, nobody bothered to fix the door. Instead, they just put a two-by-four across it about three feet from the sidewalk, which didn't make any sense because you could jump over it easily enough, unless you were a girl, in which case you could still jump over it, although you would probably show a little cheesecake in—— Why, Jack Hellman! So that's why you put that two-by-four across your office door.

This Jack Hellman writes a fine column for the *Daily Variety* and he sits there inside that open door, watching Hollywood and its joys and tribulations, as you might say, very much like Scattergood Baines sitting on his front porch—whittlin', spittin' and thinkin'. I frequently passed Scattergood Hellman's open door on account of I lived up the street a ways and I happened to pass it one morning just as Jack had run afoul of a bit of info about a remarkable young advertising man named John Bates who was in town shopping very quietly for a radio program for Canada Dry.

Jack yelled at me through the door and I

vaulted lightly over the two-by-four the way Crappy Crawford used to take the high hurdles back in Mason City High School, picked myself up off the floor, and said, "Hiya, Jackson—what's on your mind?"

Well, it seems Jack had heard our Maxwell House summer replacement and so he told me about John Bates, and within twenty-four hours this remarkable young man had recommended my show for Canada Dry. Although the Maxwell House summer show had proved that I could at least talk and also that it was possible to dress up a musical show with a lot of stuff more interesting than "And now to whisk you away for a wisp of a while from the cares of the workaday world," John Bates stuck his neck out a mile, as what I was selling him was, to a great extent, an untried theory.

Just the same, we went back on the air with it in September and did we have our share of birth pains, and believe me, I really began to appreciate George Burns's unhysterical Thursday-afternoon "Can we move?"

Our budget allowed for a singing group of two girls and three boys and I suddenly thought maybe they could also do some unison speaking in the commercials—sort of Greek-chorus style—and John God-love-him Bates said, "Let's try it. My neck couldn't be out any farther than it already is," and what happened was a lot of trial and error till we had something that sounded pretty good: five people who could speak casually but in perfect unison just like one person. In the beginning we rehearsed till we couldn't talk any more and still we weren't together, or we sounded "precious," like "Mary had a lit-tow lamb."

Then I tried writing out all the parts in musical rhythms like this:

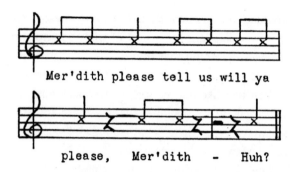

Mer'dith please tell us will ya
please, Mer'dith - Huh?

and it worked, and just reading the stuff off the paper like that, the "casual" quality began to come through and it killed all the people. We slipped the sales message right in, in the same style, and every week it got better and all we needed then was a name. For a gag, we called the act *The Talking People*, and New York City College gave us the award of the year for the best commercials, which I didn't know about till I read it in Joel Murcott's column in one of the local trade papers, which was not unusual because Hollywood always knows the details of your business, social, and private life considerably before you know them yourself.

And the *Hooper* started climbing. Now this was more like it. *Now* when I walked into the Derby everybody said hello *first*. In Hollywood that's very important. They say that Orientals bow and hiss at each other to establish which of them is the most celebrated. The fellow who stops bowing first is the inferior. In Hollywood the one who says hello first is the bit player, and the one who waits out all comers is the star. Of course, in rare cases, politeness and being brought up properly enter into it to confuse the statistics. But not often.

Anyhow, now that my own show was really on its way, the general tone of my standing in our little community, it seemed to me, was considerably raised. And to climb the capax, as my Uncle Charlie used to say, I got married. Well, what do you think happened next? The cream from the top of the cream of all the stars and big important people not only from Hollywood but also from New York and places like Florida were being invited to *the* affair to end all affairs—the Robert Montgomerys' twentieth wedding anniversary— and holy jumping jeepers for criminy sakes creepers we were invited. What an opportunity to show off to my bride what kind of an important fellow she married! Nothing succeeds like success, it never rains but it pours, everything comes to he who, him who, he who, him who, and was I proud!

Since the war there have been darn few formal affairs and so in Hollywood the invitations invariably read "black tie" or "formal" if you are expected to dress up. Believe me, I read every word on this gorgeous pasteboard and made a strong mental note that it didn't say anything about dressing. I met my bride halfway down the block as she was returning home from shopping to tell her the news and of course she said, "What do we wear?" And I said, "No dinner clothes." The unerring instinct of woman spoke up and said, "Are you sure?" And I hunted high and low for an hour to prove it. But that invitation had gone—disappeared—evaporated. However, I was sure, so we didn't check with anyone else, and came the great night we started out fashionably late for the famous Crystal Room in the Beverly Hills Hotel where this party of parties was being given. Rini tried to talk me out of wearing my new Windsor tie with the red stripes, but it looked so nice with my blue serge that I stuck with it.

The cameras and flashlights were clicking and flashing in the lobby and just ahead of us were Robert Taylor in a rather formal topcoat and Barbara Stanwyck in jewels, also Eric Johnston, Irene Dunne and her husband, and the Samuel Goldwyns in similar conditions. "Must be going to a different party," I whispered. Rini nodded, but she was slightly pale and I knew that she knew that I knew both our stomachs had turned completely over with the positive conviction that there was no other party. From then on we moved automatically toward our doom with the slow inevitability of two sleepwalkers fending off closed doors and dangerous obstructions but with a red tie and a Peter Pan collar sticking out in front instead of the usual outstretched arms.

We floated past the checkroom and then clearly saw the worst through the wide double doors—the double, triple, quadruple worst—a gleaming, snowy, immaculate receiving line shimmering and glowing, with Mr. Montgomery at the head in white tie and tails. I must have said *something* as we went down that glittering avenue—after all, I remember managing "Hod-a-do" when I shook hands with President Coolidge once—but if either Rini or I spoke at all, I have no recollection of it. The next thing I knew we were standing in a far corner of the bar overlooking the most gorgeously decorated fifty dinner tables you can imagine.

Through a haze of gibbering small talk I remember a formidable bosom saying, "No, of course the invitation didn't say white tie. It didn't have to—after all, it was *engraved.*" Just then a maître de came up and said, "You are at table ten with Mr. and Mrs. Gary Cooper, Mr. and Mrs. Kay Kyser, and Mr. and Mrs. Ray Milland." Rini said, "For two cents we ought to go home and change," and we immediately started thinking in this direction. Our first problem was that we couldn't face the thought of going back past the receiving line—that would be too obvious. But right at our elbow was a door and, as one so often does the handy thing, rather than the reasonable thing, we stepped through this door and found ourselves in the kitchen. After dodging chefs and cooks and waiters for a few minutes, I took two highballs from a passing tray in desperation, and this gave me an idea. Nobody goes home with a full drink in his hand, so all we had to do was walk sort of backward past the welcoming group at the door as though we had some temporary business in the lobby, give the drinks to the elevator starter, and scram. Everything worked fine if you can call any of this fine until I realized that it would take me half the night to find our car, so, Saturday night or not, we had to hunt up a taxi. All this time I was cussing myself for being an idiot and why make such a simple thing so important and wouldn't I ever grow up and how ridiculous to rush around in a sopping sweat, frantic and gulping, just like that evening at the banquet in the Great Hall in Mason City High School over a quarter of a century ago. But none of this reflection did either of us any good at all and presently we were in a taxi heading for home a half-hour away covered with prickly heat from head to foot, calculating how long it would take us to get dressed and back to the party and would my tails still fit and was Rini's evening dress pressed and did I have a clean collar and where were my studs?

Then forty or fifty years later we finally arrived home and I was telling the driver to turn around and be ready for the dash back to the hotel. Rini had meanwhile unbuttoned all of her buttons to save time and we rushed to the front door. I reached for my keys—and I would have found them, too, if they hadn't been stuck in the ignition of the car fifteen miles away in the Beverly Hills Hotel parking lot. . . .

Twenty years hence, I know we will only have to close our eyes to hear the sound of that taxi chugging futilely in our driveway, only the memory will probably make us shriek with laughter instead of shudder with horror as we did during that incredible moment. The *sounds* don't change in our memories—only the perspective.

Sounds like the soft, slow putt-putt of the one-cylinder White Pier launch, the noisy oarlock on Mr. Stratton's green rowboat, the reedy buzz a blade of grass makes when you blow on it between your thumbs, the screech of the Clear Lake interurban coming around the corner into Clear Lake's Main Street, and all the wonderful procedure of the conductor, Mr. Seissiger, as Mama gave him the money and he reached overhead to grab the wooden grip on the rod that went all the way along the ceiling of the car to the cash-register clock in the back. He'd click the rod around past the local five cents, past the ten cents trip to the greenhouse, and past the "transfer" slot, clear to the twenty-five cents marker at the bottom—we were going all the way—and then he'd pull the slack fare rope in that professional way of his, sort of down and then a little flourish to the side, and you'd hear the register ring up and you were relieved that he didn't ask for a fare for you, because even though you'd squeeze down, you were beginning to look a little too old to ride for nothing.

Your first view of the lake waiting for you at the foot of the street was always so exciting every summer. Funny I never remembered the interurban screech around that corner going home. Going home was exciting, too, though—first the brickyards, then the Odd Fellows' Home, then the Junction, then the ball park, then the fair grounds, then the viaduct, then the Main Street Bridge, then Home.

A small-town kid also gets to go to sleep every night with a train whistle way off—even the engine shoof-shoof-shoofing sounds pretty clear at night in a small town.

If I ever write another symphony, I'd like to take a crack at something that would include all the promises of the train whistle and engine shoofing. The promises and dreams are in many ways more wonderful than the fulfillments.

Sure, I'll trade you Ed Patchen and Squiz Hazelton for Sousa and Toscanini, and Mr. Bushgens for Dr. Lee De Forest, Roger Glanville for Benton and Bowles, and the Rose Theatre in the cellar for the San Francisco Opera House, Clear Lake for the Pacific Ocean, and "Aunt" Marie for a good Hooper rating. Sure, I'll trade, but only temporarily. . . .

L'Envoi IN THE MEANTIME I'VE taken on tailor-made suits, five of them all at once, also notified my dentist to expect me four times a year instead of twice, and over at the barbershop Harry has me down for the full treatment every seven days, instead of once a month. I also plan to tee up my own golf balls on the practice range, starting tomorrow, eat lettuce for breakfast, cottage cheese for lunch, Ry-krisp for dinner, and half a grapefruit before and after every meal.

Television, you know.

You're darn tootin' I keep the piccolo shined up.

MEREDITH WILLSON (1902–1984) was a musician, composer, songwriter, conductor, and playwright. Best known for the Broadway musicals *Meredith Willson's The Music Man* and *The Unsinkable Molly Brown*, he also wrote several autobiographical books, including *Eggs I Have Laid* and *"But He Doesn't Know the Territory"* (Minnesota, 2009).